Time in India's Development Programmes

Harvard Economic Studies / Volume 137

The studies in this series are published by the Department of Economics of Harvard University. The Department does not assume responsibility for the views expressed.

Time in India's Development Programmes

Robert C. Repetto

Harvard University Press / Cambridge, Massachusetts

1971

© Copyright 1971 by the President and Fellows of Harvard College
All rights reserved
Distributed in Great Britain by Oxford University Press, London
Library of Congress Catalog Card Number 71-143230
SBN 674-89180-5
Printed in the United States of America

Acknowledgements

This study is a revised version of a doctoral dissertation submitted
to the Department of Economics of Harvard University in 1967.
Of the numerous people who supported and assisted in the work,
I would like to acknowledge in particular the support of Dr.
Douglas Ensminger, former Representative of the Ford Founda-
tion in India; Mr. Morton Grossman, then Ford Foundation
Specialist in Economic Planning in India; and Professor Edward
Mason of Harvard University. I am also indebted to Mr. Satish
Chandra, Managing Director, and other officers of the Fertiliser
Corporation of India for their cooperation in the work under-
lying Chapter 3. Chapter 4 bears the imprint of Mr. Ellis Hatt,
then Consultant in Water Management to the Ford Foundation
in India, and rests on the intelligent assistance of Professor Tilak
Raj of the Department of Agricultural Economics, Punjab Agricultural University, and Mr. Gurdev Singh Sidhu of the Punjab
Extension Service. Professor S. Johl and Dr. Charles Moore of
the Punjab Agricultural University also provided generous and
valuable assistance. I am also indebted to Drs. Peter King, H.
Bradley Wells, Jason Finkle, and Mr. Eugene Weiss, all formerly
with the Ford Foundation in India, for assistance in the study of
family planning.

Contents

Tables

Time in India's Development Programmes

1 Preliminary Issues and Summary

In India, and in the developing world as a whole, most of the increasing flow of investment needed for sustained rapid income growth must come from domestic sources. For success in mobilising these domestic resources, a higher rate of return on investment is crucial. Larger returns induce both upward shifts in the domestic savings function and rapid movements along it. Along with improvements on traditional technology, improvements in resource allocation can be important in raising the overall rate of return on investment. In India, as in other developing countries, there are considerable opportunities to economise more effectively in the use of scarce resources. Realisation of these opportunities could create an important source of accelerated growth.

This study is concerned with greater economy in the use of capital, India's scarcest resource. Economising on the use of capital means, essentially, the application of appropriate rates of time discount in making economic decisions of all kinds. In the consideration of alternative courses of action, due weight should be given to present relative to future consumption levels.

If the appropriate rates of time discount are relatively high, actions are favoured which reduce the gestation periods and foreshorten the time stream of returns on investments and which make intensive use of the means already at hand.

There can be little doubt but that in India the appropriate rates of time discount are relatively high. If the masses live near the margin of subsistence, then postponement of consumption involves a considerable sacrifice. The poverty of most Indians imposes a mode of life which permits the purchase of simple food, clothing, shelter, and very little else. There are few items in the budgets of most Indian families, even of those well up in the income scale, consumption of which can be postponed. The contrast with the affluent societies, in which only a modest fraction of personal consumption expenditure is devoted to the necessities of life, is striking.

It is also widely considered that in India and much of the developing world generally the prospects are good for rates of economic growth more rapid than those being sustained in the advanced countries. This expectation is based largely on the possibilities of rapid technological change, as the techniques and knowledge gradually accumulated in the developed countries are adapted and applied.

The combination of extremely low present levels of consumption and a relatively high expected growth rate creates a strong presumption that future consumption should be discounted rather heavily. This remains so regardless of the existence of various imperfections in capital and other markets, which affect the level of market interest rates,[1] or of externalities in consumption which could cause the appropriate social rate of time discount to depart from market rates.[2]

The determination of social rates of time preference is an extremely complex problem, on which considerable analytical but little empirical work has as yet been accomplished.[3] This study is not devoted to that problem. Rather, it is an exploration of the effects of more consistent application of discount factors, taking for granted that there is considerable scope in rapidly modernising economies partially insulated from the forces of competition, for improvements in efficiency at the level of the enterprise, the industry, and the sector. Often, it appears, the question is less whether a rate of 6 percent or 8 percent has been used in arriving at a decision than whether any positive rate has been applied at all.

In this study, calculations have been performed with a range of time discount rates from 7 to 15 percent. This should be generally accepted as a reasonable range of values for the Indian economy in the 1960's. None of the economic comparisons or the major conclusions are qualitatively altered by the use of the lower, instead of the higher, figure; the differences are those of degree. The finding of considerable opportunities for improvements in allocative efficiency at the micro-level implies considerable scope for accelerated growth out of internal resources. This conclusion, specifically with reference to the management of time in development programmes, is brought to bear on some leading issues of development economics: investment strategy, the determinants of comparative advantage, the choice of techniques, and the nature of infant industry economies.

The empirical work in the following chapters has involved numerous benefit-cost comparisons. The criterion employed has generally been the discounted present value of the activities, normalised for differences in scale as measured by the value of output. However, in certain chapters, as noted in the text, the structure of the data has necessitated a different normalisation procedure, with implications which have been explained.

Costs and benefits have been evaluated at market prices, from the standpoint of the enterprise. This procedure does not imply belief in the fulfillment of all the conditions of perfect competition. Obviously, in India as in other countries, numerous departures from this ideal have been introduced by market imperfections and the distorting effects of government policy. Nevertheless, the use of market prices, as a matter of general principle, rests on two considerations which seem fundamental.

The primary consideration is the decentralisation of economic decision-making. The Indian economy is generally considered to be more centrally planned than are most in the developing world. Yet, the effect of private decisions on the allocation of resources is overwhelmingly dominant and, even within the public sector, the diffusion of responsibility for economic decisions is extremely broad. The influence on the development programme of engineers, accountants, purchase officers, and administrators at all organisational levels is great. Accordingly, the process of economic development is not just the adoption of more sophisticated techniques of planning and project evaluation by the planning agencies; it is rather more the acquisition of attitudes and skills within innumerable enterprises throughout the economy which lead to more effective use of resources. The problems and skills involved in suboptimisation by the enterprise within a market environment are themselves extensive and complex, as the curriculum of any business administration course attests. The potential gains in productivity are large. It should be an important objective of economic policy to create a market environment conducive to the acquisition and exercise of these managerial skills.

For the private sector, which in any case will be guided by profit considerations, this objective demands efforts to create an environment in which private profits are determined by skill in seizing market opportunities and in economising on inputs rather than skill in manipulating the governmental administrative machinery. The use of accounting prices different from market prices by official agencies engaged in the approval or disapproval of private economic decisions inevitably involves those agencies in attempts to override the profit incentive with administrative controls. Such attempts impose heavy costs: the civil service is overly burdened and demoralised, and businessmen find it more profitable to lobby than to manage, while controls inevitably are increasingly eroded or evaded anyhow. An effective and appropriate economic policy is one which reconciles private and social costs through the price mechanism. Therefore, should there be a distortion in market prices which is temporarily beyond the power of the government to repair, it is preferable, in all probability, that enterprises continue to develop the skills of the marketplace, even at the cost of some misallocation, and that the government conserve its administrative resources for more fruitful tasks than control.

It is often thought that shadow prices can operate more effectively within the public sector, so long as enterprise managers and subordinates are aware that their performance will be evaluated on the basis of accounting prices. There are several reasons why this is not altogether true in fact. Government is rarely united on the overall advisability of the change in policy to which the shadow price corresponds; if it were, there would be no need to resort to half measures like shadow pricing. As a result, the enterprise manager and his subordinates are subjected to conflicting demands. The planning commission may urge that wage rates be "shadowed" downwards and foreign exchange be

5

"shadowed" upwards. However, at the same time, the finance ministry is likely to be upbraiding the enterprise for its low return on the public funds entrusted to it and the government auditor will be questioning the enterprise's chief purchase officer on his failure to accept a low bid for some materials. Faced with these conflicting pressures, public sector enterprises will not base their decisions consistently on shadow prices.

In many developing countries, the executive ministries and public corporations are powerful organisations with considerable political influence, having well-established traditions, bureaucracies, and engineering elites. The economic planning authorities are generally dependent on them for the formulation and preparation of new investment projects, as well as for plan implementation. The planning authorities are likely to be only moderately successful in determining the final selection of investment projects, should serious differences of opinion exist, and largely without direct influence over their conception and design. Furthermore, within the public sector enterprises organisational considerations are strong. The need for efficiency must be constantly asserted against the claims of safety, convenience, ambition, and the sanctity of established procedure. The budgetary constraint is the most effective means by which the need for efficiency can be made tangible throughout the public sector. Scarcities must be felt as costs which limit the organisation's activities. Consequently, it is no less important for the public sector than for the private that economic policy be transmitted through the price mechanism. Within the public sector as well, decision-making authority is decentralised, there is considerable scope for better suboptimisation, and the enterprises respond to profit and budget incentives which are based on market prices.

The second fundamental consideration which favours adherence to market prices in evaluating benefits and costs is simply recognition that government policy is what it is, until it is changed. A typical list of market failures in developing countries allegedly justifying shadow pricing contains items, the large majority of which are amenable to government action, e.g., the presence of external effects, natural or contrived monopolies, currency overvaluation, protective devices like tariffs or import quotas, an inflated industrial wage rate, unemployment and underemployment, a deficiency of savings, imperfect capital markets, a maldistribution of income and wealth, and exaggerated private uncertainty and risk allowances.[4] Government policy deals extensively with external effects through subsidy (education, free inoculations), taxes (on liquor), and regulation (zoning laws). It deals with natural monopolies (nationalisation or regulation) and artificial ones (protection, price controls, industrial licensing). The government influences industrial wage rates through wage legislation, intervention in collective bargaining and trade union legislation, and provision of subsidised worker housing or foodstuffs. The government intervenes in capital markets through regulation or the creation of financial institutions. Government directly controls exchange rates, tariffs, and import quotas. Through its taxing powers, the government influences the distribution of income and wealth; this, along with the government's own operation, largely determines propensities to save. Finally, government affects private risk-perception and uncertainty through extension services, forecasting, insurance, and joint ventures.

It is evident that governments typically display concern over these problems of market failure and have policies directed towards their resolution. These policies may not be those which would appeal to any particular group of outside economists or even those which the planning commission would like to have

7

adopted. Probably, government policies will be neither systematic nor altogether consistent, since policy changes tend to be gradual and piecemeal. Nonetheless, it would be unrealistic to assume that policies are simply whimsical or the result of a random historical process. Policy decisions emerge as the resultant of economic, political, and administrative forces acting on the government. Thus when economists state, in representing a deficiency of savings as a structural defect, that "the government may not be willing or able to tax more heavily," this implies that the government views the added administrative costs and overall political opposition involved in raising new taxation as exceeding the extra worth to society of additional goods available for consumption in a future period. This, then, is current social policy as formulated by the responsible political authority. It is not immutable, and all its implications may not even be fully understood by the policy makers. Economists may well succeed, by laying bare these implications and delineating an attractive alternative, in influencing the government to adopt a different policy. But, economists cannot, in the name of social cost-benefit analysis, simply put aside these official positions without substituting arbitrary and irresponsible political judgements of their own.

Of course, there is no bar against political advocacy by economists, whether they are working in a planning commission or elsewhere. But, some may think it more forthright and effective to cast such advocacy in a form less oblique than the suggestion of shadow prices. Because of the diffusion of decision-making authority and the lack of a strong consensus within the government, shadow prices are unlikely to influence the allocation of resources significantly unless supported by taxes and subsidies, or debilitating controls. Such fiscal supports are often equivalent in scope and effect to the desired change in policy itself, so that the government may be as easily persuaded to adopt the latter as the former. For example, were it possible to persuade government to impose a uniform tax on all foreign exchange purchases and grant a similar subsidy on all foreign exchange sales, in support of a shadow price for foreign exchange, it would certainly be possible to persuade government to change the official exchange rate. Or, on the other hand, should conditions within a society strongly discourage attempts to redistribute income through the revenue budget, it seems unlikely that significant redistribution would be possible through the expenditure budget: if those adversely affected were so influential initially, they would probably be able to offset in large part the effects of a changed pattern of expenditures through changes in the means of financing those expenditures.[5] In general, it is strongly arguable that economists should attempt to bring about policy changes they consider desirable and, in the interim, accept the policy framework which exists as a basis for analysis.

This position would be weakened if the allocation of resources were greatly affected by truly structural defects beyond the potential powers of government to remedy for a long time. Recent literature on the problems of the "labour-surplus economy" has emphasised the implications of downwardly rigid real wage rates and an unshakable ˋconnection between the levels of consumption and employment. Under these conditions the operation of the market economy would lead to economic growth at the maximum feasible rate and minimum levels of consumption and employment.[6] Under these conditions, should present consumption have any social value in itself, there would be a case for government intervention in support of additional employment. The assumption of institutionally fixed real wage rates in developing countries is derived from the long and inconclusive literature on the existence of "disguised unemployment." It is

somewhat difficult to understand the mechanism by which money
wage rates, let alone real wage rates, are institutionally fixed
in economies predominantly rural and atomistic. Indeed, in
the relatively small organised sector, wage rates may be rigid, but
this is largely the result of government action, not a problem
beyond its reach. For the rest of the economy, the most plausible
rationale for this assumption is that there exists a basically com-
munal form of land tenure under which each rural worker receives
essentially his average product.[7] Thus, industrial wage rates must
at least equal labour's average product in agriculture, substantially
exceeding the marginal product and leading to underemployment.
While this rationale may have some applicability, it is contradicted
by the widespread existence of market transactions in agricultural
land and labour. Urban-rural wage differentials can readily be
explained by differences in real living costs, dislocation costs,
differences in the productivity of a stable industrial worker, or
by the effects of union or governmental action. Perhaps before
sweeping policy conclusions are accepted, more empirical investigation of the relevant labour market behaviour is desirable.

It is probable that the position just outlined would be rejected
at the present time by many economists interested in economic
development, although most would undoubtedly consider it a
possible one. In any case, these views are not central to the thesis
which follows but are introduced in explanation of the use of
market prices in making economic comparisons. Probably, the
central conclusions would still emerge if another system were
adopted.

Chapter 2 suggests that one of the most important implications
of high rates of time discount for investment policy is that capital
projects must be completed and brought into full production in

the shortest possible time. It suggests that, in view of the past experience of India and other developing countries, improvements in this area would have a very considerable effect in raising the return on investment and may often provide the margin of competitiveness in import substitution or exporting. In this light, the costs of unbalanced growth seem inordinate, and the requirements for balanced growth place a premium on flexibility and decentralisation in planning.

Chapter 3 builds on the preceding to advance the hypothesis that one of the more significant forms of learning experience associated with infant industry economies may be the growth in competence within an industry to plan, implement, and bring into full production new investment projects without costly delays. Realisation of the potential benefits of establishing a domestically based industry and expansion of "absorptive capacity" will depend critically on the degree of success in overcoming transitional difficulties in this area. This hypothesis was explored by means of a detailed study of the experience of a large public sector corporation in the fertiliser industry. The results indicate the importance of policies and organisational changes to shorten the learning period, and the importance of increased control over project schedules compared to other potential economies associated with greater domestic experience and participation in the investment process.

Chapter 4 uses studies carried out in the field of irrigation in India to elaborate critical factors in the choice of technique. The results emphasise that gestation periods are of the essence of capital intensity and that differences in the time-streams of benefits will usually be the determining factor in sectors which offer large potential payoffs. For alternative means of irrigation

11

in India, the results show that the high rates of discount place a premium on steps to raise the productivity of existing works and on new schemes which can be quickly developed.

Chapter 5 uses the results of a study of the Madras vasectomy programme in India to suggest again the importance, in programmes with large potential returns, of measures to accelerate the time-stream of benefits. The study of this family planning programme suggests that manipulation of private incentives and the involvement of private initiative can often successfully complement administrative efforts and lead to fast results when administrative capacity is constrained. The results also suggest the usefulness of even crude decision models when programmes are surrounded with uncertainty and risk, in order to reduce the length of decision lags.

Chapter 6, the concluding chapter, is a crude attempt to assess the potential impact on Indian growth of possible improvements in productivity in the areas studied in the preceding chapters. The results suggest that throughout the economy such internal changes might do much to close the gap between desired and actual rates of growth in per capita income.

2 Gestation Lags and the Rate of Return
to Investment

Chapter 1 has suggested that the extremely low level of income in India implies a low rate of substitution of future for present consumption. This, and the expectation of relatively rapid future income growth, create a presumption that social rates of time discount are relatively high. This emphasises the importance of obtaining maximal returns from investments and puts a heavy weight on the returns obtainable during the early years of a project life. Yet, in India, as in many other developing countries, one encounters large sums tied up in projects with extended gestation periods, widespread and considerable lags in project completion, and substantial underutilisation of both new and existing facilities. These phenomena represent a large loss to the nation in potential income and potential savings for reinvestment; they also represent a reserve of unrealised capability for accelerated growth through internal improvements in the operation of the economy. This chapter is primarily an attempt to show the possible magnitude of this reserve and to draw some conclusions on project selection and investment planning.

Chapter 3 is concerned with the causes underlying this problem and measures devised to eliminate it in one Indian industry. Many of the causes, however, transcend the limits of a single industry, and lie in the basic framework of economic planning. There is a strong humanitarian, nationalistic, and political impetus in India to plan and budget for the maximal use of resources that are and will be available through the growth process. Despite the vagaries of nature and the uncertainties of the world climate, there has been little allowance in the past for adverse "shocks" to the economy or for the cost and schedule overruns that seem inevitably to occur in a large percentage of projects. Within this taut budgetary framework, resources have been committed to large projects at an early stage, through either foreign credits or domestic budgetary allocations, often on the basis of tentative and optimistic data on costs and demand levels, schedules, and so on. This early commitment of resources to projects with long gestation periods, to which foreign aid procedures have contributed in no small measure, reduced considerably the flexibility required in the planning mechanism to adjust to changing circumstances. In this context, delays in the completion of infrastructure projects and those in key import-replacing or export-producing sectors have increased the pressure on the balance of payments and domestic resources. Adherence to outmoded targets and some lack of capability to rephase and adjust projects and programmes throughout the economy with sufficient speed has reinforced this inflexibility and pressure on resources. One response has been a heavy reliance on direct controls over foreign exchange payments, investment allocations, and critical materials, in order to increase the "bite" of adjustment policies and to concentrate cuts on sectors which might have a high private profitability but which are thought to be of low social priority. The operation of such controls, however, over an increasingly well-knit and interdependent domestic economy in a deteriorating resource position

TABLE 1. Gestation Periods in Major Public Sector Projects: First, Second, and Third Plan Periods, in Months

Industry	Average length of period[a]					
	Approval in principle to receipt of detailed project report	Detailed project report to final gov't approval	Final approval to start of construction	Start of construction to start of commercial production	Total lag behind initially scheduled production start	Commercial production start to full capacity operations
Five fertiliser projects	24 (3)	3 (3)	27 (5)	45 (5)	30 (5)	30 (2)
Four refinery projects	n.a.	n.a.	n.a.	33 (3)	12 (4)	12 (2)
Ten thermal power generating projects	18 (2)	12 (8)	9 (8)	39 (10)	15 (10)	9 (6)
Twelve engineering and machinery projects	15 (8)	6 (8)	9 (9)	24 (11)	12 (6)	63 (12)[b]
Five coal washeries	24 (4)	18 (4)[c]	n.a.	33 (5)[d]	12 (4)	48 (2)
Five steel projects[e]	12 (5)	9 (5)	6 (4)	30 (4)[f]	9 (5)[f]	36 (3)[f]

Sources: Various annual reports of ministries, public sector companies, annual reports on the working of public sector enterprises, and planning commission documents.

a The number of projects included in each average is given in parentheses.
b Partially estimated.
c Notice inviting tender to major contract award.
d Contract award to production start.
e Including two expansions.
f Refers to finished steel.

15

proved ever more difficult. The problem of apportioning inadequate resources among increasingly numerous, diverse, and interrelated claimants has itself contributed to delays. Market prices and responses have been distorted, complicating the task of forward planning and promoting inefficient uses of resources. Imbalances have arisen in a number of industries between productive capacity and the inputs to utilise it or the demands in industries which consume the product, leading to considerable excess capacity. Broadly speaking these factors and the transitional problems, discussed in the next chapter, of learning by experience to plan and manage large industrial projects, have created substantial reserves of potential income growth to be mobilised through reductions in gestation periods and lags in key projects, avoidance of premature commitment of resources, and acceleration of the time-streams of benefits through fuller and faster utilisation of new and existing capacities.

Table 1 presents some illustrative material to indicate the broad magnitudes of gestation periods and gestation lags that have affected major industrial investments in the public sector. Such summary data are inherently crude in both concept and measurement and are introduced only to give a sense of dimension. Private sector projects have been excluded, not because schedule overruns and protracted gestation periods are restricted to the government sector but because the "accountability" of the latter generates more information. The one available survey of seventy-five private industrial investment projects has indicated that significant delays in the start of production affected no less than 75 percent of the respondents, with the average delay between seven and eight months.[1]

Table 2 provides further indication of the extent of these gestation periods and illustrates one major consequence, namely,

TABLE 2. Annual Authorisation and Utilisation of Foreign Assistance, 1958-1959 to 1965-1966

Year of authorisation	Amount, Rs Crore[a]	Percent utilised by 3/31/1961	Percent utilised in				
			1961-62	1962-63	1963-64	1964-65	1965-66
1958-59							
Non-project	176	72	14	9	1	-	-
Project	126	86	6	2	4	2	-
1959-60							
Non-project	48	66	12	11	4	6	-
Project	262	11	4	9	14	22	19
1960-61							
Non-project	130	47	18	12	15	5	1
Project	185	4	33	7	8	14	7
1961-62							
Non-project	106	-	80	5	3	4	4
Project	270	-	4	21	22	24	15
1962-63							
Non-project	290	-	-	33	26	28	8
Project	317	-	-	3	24	28	13
1963-64							
Non-project	189	-	-	-	16	34	35
Project	238	-	-	-	2	20	23
1964-65							
Non-project	134	-	-	-	-	33	48
Project	331	-	-	-	-	5	15

Sources: From GOI, Ministry of Finance, *External Assistance*, various years, *Economic Survey*, various years, and Reserve Bank of India, *Annual Survey*, various years.

[a]One crore equals 10 million.

the slow pattern of utilisation of foreign credits tied to investment projects. Typically, such credit arrangements are concluded at an early stage of project development—before equipment orders are placed and sometimes before detailed project study has been undertaken. Foreign capital availability, especially on concessionary terms, is limited in amount to India, and to a degree credits committed to particular projects are unavailable for other purposes. (In some circumstances, of course, capital is available *only* for a particular project and substitution possibilities are nil.) Therefore, with high implicit rates of time discount, a substantial social cost is incurred when available capital is unutilised for considerable periods. The figures,[2] which must be read with the explanatory footnote for an understanding of the coverage and concepts employed, indicate that the magnitudes and duration of this underutilisation have been considerable during the Third Plan period, which has been a matter of grave concern to the Government of India.[3]

It is more difficult to present meaningful data on the extent of underutilised capacity in India, to say nothing of the problems of distinguishing planned versus unplanned overcapacity and of determining the causative factors. Even in more developed industrial countries like the United States, statistics on capacity and capacity utilisation leave much to be desired. In India, there are additional conceptual and empirical problems.[4] Nonetheless, both official data and the large number of partial studies available indicate that the degree of unutilised industrial capacity has been large over a wide range of industries and a considerable period of time.[5] Aside from local managerial and labour problems, much of it can be attributed to imbalances and lack of synchronisation: on the aggregate level, between the pace of investment and the growth in the economy's ability to supply maintenance imports; on the industrial level, between the growth of capacities in producing and consuming sectors; on the project level, between the completion of various installations in interrelated complexes.

The following calculations are intended to show that the costs of these underutilised resources are a major source of inadequate returns to investment; or, to put it more positively, that the reserves of productive potential comprise an extremely promising source of internally generated economic growth. A relatively simple discounted cash flow analytical framework has been developed in order to demonstrate the effects of more rapid project completion and attainment of full capacity production on the net worth of the individual enterprise. The variables that enter the model are as follows:

X = full-capacity physical output rate, or volume index, per year

k = the total capital cost of the project per unit of output at full capacity production

p = the unit value price of output

c = direct variable operating costs per unit of output

C = total operating costs which do not vary with output, i.e., fixed costs

r = the marginal efficiency of capital, or social rate of time discount

A = the time at which production begins, measured from the start of investment outlay

L = the time at which production ceases, measured from A

V = the discounted present value of the project

$f(t)$ = the time distribution of investment outlay

$g(t)$ = the time profile of output

j = the percentage of investment outlay which occurs before production can begin

Then, assuming that parameter values would be chosen to make $f(t)$ almost zero well before t=L the expression for V is approximately

1) $$V = \int_{A}^{A+L} (p-c)Xg(t)e^{-rt}dt - \int_{A}^{A+L} Ce^{-rt}dt - \int_{0}^{\infty} kXf(t)e^{-rt}dt$$

A flexible and convenient form of the function $f(t)$ is the gamma function, which assumes a unimodal distribution of investment outlay over time:

2) $$f(t) = \frac{b^{n+1}}{n!} \, t^n \, e^{-bt}$$

which implies that

3) $$\int_{0}^{\infty} f(t)e^{-rt}dt = \frac{b^{n+1}}{(b+r)^{n+1}}$$

As a specification for the function $g(t)$ an appropriate form would be a logistics-type relation which approaches unity as t increases:

4) $$g(t) = 1 - e^{-a(t-A)}$$

5) $$\int_{A}^{A+L} g(t)e^{-rt}dt = \frac{e^{-ra}}{r(r+a)} \, [re^{-rL}(e^{-aL}-1)-a(e^{-rL}-1)]$$

If one is willing to ignore a term as small as $re^{-(r+A)L}$, which should be very close to zero, then

6) $$\int_{A}^{A+L} g(t)e^{-rt}dt = \frac{e^{-rA}}{r(r+a)} \, [a-(a+r)e^{-rL}]$$

and the whole expression can be rewritten as

7) $$V = \frac{(p-c)e^{-rA}(a-(a+r)e^{-rL})X}{r(r+a)} - \frac{Ce^{-rA}(1-e^{-rL})}{r} - \frac{kX b^{n+1}}{(b+r)^{n+1}}$$

The start-up time A must be considered to be a function of the parameters of $f(t)$, such that production begins the sooner, the sooner the investiment is completed. For purposes of analysis, it can be assumed that production begins after a specified fraction of the investment has been completed.

8) $\qquad \int_0^A f(t)dt = j \qquad\qquad 0 < j \leq 1$

This determines A, given $f(t)$ and j. It would be useful to express V directly in terms of the start-up time A: from 2) and 8) it can be derived that

9) $\qquad \frac{\partial A}{\partial b} = -\frac{A}{b}$, and so

10) $\quad Ab = x$, where x is a constant of integration. If one considers only integral values of n, this constant follows the relationship

11) $\quad j = 1 - e^{-x} (1 + x + \frac{x^2}{2!} + \dots + \frac{x^n}{n!})$

Values of this relationship are presented for given n and j in Table 3. In later applications, only $n=2$ and $j=.75$ are used. The result is that the expression for V can be written in a final version, this time as

12) $\quad V = \frac{(p-c)Xe^{-rA} \, (a - (a+r)e^{-rL})}{r(r+a)} - \frac{Ce^{-rA} \, (1 - e^{-rL})}{r} - \frac{kX \, x^{n+1}}{(x+rA)^{n+1}}$.

From this expression it is possible to assess the impact on the discounted net worth of the project of changes in the construction period or in the period required to attain full capacity. Also, it is possible to reformulate the model slightly to encompass a wide variety of financial arrangements. For example, if all investment funds were committed at the very outset, the

TABLE 3. Calculation of the Value of x in the Relation
$$Ab = x$$

$$j = 1 - e^{-x} \left(1 + x + \frac{x^2}{2!} + \cdots + \frac{x^n}{n!}\right)$$

Value of x for values of j

n	$j = 0.75$	$j = 0.90$
1	2.65	3.89
2	3.92	5.38
3	5.10	6.75

last term of the expression would simply be $-kX$, with the rest of the relation unchanged.

In the following paragraphs, hypothetical parameter values are used to explore the impact of these gestation lags for projects of (a) different capital intensity, (b) alternative financing arrangements, and (c) different *ex ante* profitability. In all that follows, the choice of units has been such that the full-capacity physical output rate per year in each project is equal to unity (in tons, numbers, or whatever), and the price of this unit of output is also unity (in rupees). Therefore, total capital requirements, the discounted present value of the investment, and project costs will all be expressed in units corresponding to the value of one year's full capacity output. Conversion to units based on the total capital requirements of the projects is a simple matter, using the capital-output ratios. The production span of all projects has been assumed to be fifteen years, with no subsequent scrap value. The start of production has been assumed to occur after 75 percent of the total investment has been disbursed, a conservative assumption.

The simplest and conventional way of representing investment costs in such analyses is to assume that investment *costs* coincide

TABLE 4. Project Net Worth as a Function of Project Completion Date

$r = 0.07$
$C = 0.10$

$k=1$; $(1-c) = 0.24$		$k=2$; $(1-c) = 0.36$		$k=3$; $(1-c) = 0.49$	
A	V	A	V	A	V
2	0.014	2	0.03	2	0.045
3	.000	3	.00	3	.000
4	-.016	4	-.03	-4	-.045
5	-.030	5	-.06	5	-.087
6	-.042	6	-.08	6	-.125

$r = 0.15$
$C = 0.10$

$k=1$; $(1-c) = 0.34$		$k=2$; $(1-c) = 0.56$		$k=3$; $(1-c) = 0.78$	
A	V	A	V	A	V
2	0.03	2	0.07	2	0.10
3	.00	3	.00	3	.00
4	-.04	4	-.07	4	-.12
5	-.05	5	-.11	5	-.17
6	-.08	6	-.15	6	-.23

in time with investment *outlays*. Although this is not usually true from the standpoint of the individual enterprise which finances investment substantially through borrowing, it is true from the national standpoint for all investments out of *domestic* resources. Even from the national standpoint, it is not true of the foreign capital component of investment, for which the resource costs to the economy (in interest, dividend, and amortisation payments) may not coincide in time with the disbursements. The effect of this "pay-as-you-go" assumption is to minimise the cost of lags in the construction period, since

TABLE 5. Project Net Worth as a Function of Attainment of
Full Capacity Output

$r = 0.07$
$C = 0.10$

k=1; (1-c) = 0.24		k=2; (1-c) = 0.36		k=3; (1-c) = 0.49	
t: $g(t)$ = 0.85	V	t: $g(t)$ = 0.85	V	t: $g(t)$ = 0.85	V
1.5	0.03	1.5	0.06	1.5	0.07
2.0	.00	2.0	.00	2.0	.00
2.5	-.06	2.5	-.08	2.5	-.11
3.8	-.17	3.8	-.24	3.8	-.33
4.7	-.24	4.7	-.35	4.7	-.47

$r = 0.15$
$C = 0.10$

k=1; (1-c) = 0.34		k=2; (1-c) = 0.56		k=3; (1-c) = 0.78	
t: $g(t)$ = 0.85	V	t: $g(t)$ = 0.85	V	t: $g(t)$ = 0.85	V
1.5	0.03	1.5	0.05	1.5	0.07
2.0	.00	2.0	.00	2.0	.00
2.5	-.05	2.5	-.09	2.5	-.12
3.8	-.14	3.8	-.23	3.8	-.32
4.7	-.20	4.7	-.33	4.7	-.46

such lags defer both benefits and costs. Table 4 presents the
discounted net worth V as a function of the time for start-up
A, for various projects, based on the relationship (12). At
discount rates of first 7 percent and then 15 percent, the procedure has been to choose projects with capital-output ratios
k of one, two, and three in such a way that *each* would just
break even (V=0) if production began after three years. This
implies, of course, that the operating margin (1 - c) must be

much greater for more capital-using projects and at higher rates of time discount. The results show that at the lower rate of discount, a one-year lag in project completion reduces the net worth of the project by about 1.5 percent of the total capital employed; a two-year lag reduces it by about 3 percent. At a 15 percent rate of discount, the costs are about 3 percent and 6 percent of the total capital employed for lags of one and two years. While these magnitudes are not negligible, neither are they impressively large. It is interesting, however, to pursue the matter a bit further.

Delays in reaching full production after project completion, under pay-as-you-go financing, defer only the benefits and direct operating costs, and so are more damaging to net worth. In Table 5, essentially the *same* projects are reexamined for variations in this second kind of lag: whereas it was assumed previously that once completed, all projects would reach an output rate of 85 percent of capacity at the end of the second year (corresponding to $a=1$ in the distribution function $g(t) = 1 - e^{-a(t-A)}$), here it is assumed that all projects reach start-up at the end of the third year (corresponding to $A=3$) and the period required to reach full capacity varies. For greater intelligibility, the function $g(t)$ is described in Table 5 in terms of only one characteristic: the length of time needed to reach 85 percent of the full-capacity output rate. The correspondence between this and values of the parameter a is illustrated below.

Value of a	Value of t; $g(t) = 0.85$	Value of $g(t)$; $t = 2$
1.25	1.5	0.91
1.00	2.0	.85
0.85	2.2	.82
0.75	2.5	.78
0.50	3.8	.63
0.40	4.7	.55

For $a = 0.50$, for example, production at the end of the second year of operations runs at 63 percent of capacity, and it takes 3.8 years to reach 85 percent of capacity, and so on.

The results show that delays in reaching full capacity have a substantial impact on the net value of projects at all capital intensities and both high and low rates of discount. A delay of only six months reduces the present value by 4 to 6 percent of total capital employed; a delay of two years reduces it by 12 to 17 percent. Taken together, Tables 4 and 5 demonstrate that, even under these simplest assumptions, changes in the time required to complete projects and get them into full production have important effects on investment returns. In fact, however, the assumption that investment costs coincide with investment outlays is unrealistic for the larger part of India's development projects. Foreign credits have financed a considerable share of India's investments in industry and infrastructure. The availability of such credit is limited, and the financial terms are, in most instances, lower than the marginal efficiency of capital in India. For proper resource allocation, this portion of project costs should be charged at the time at which capital is committed and made unavilable for other purposes. If this were done in practice, the real costs to the economy of the pattern of early commitment and slow utilisation brought out in Table 2 would be more evident.

Tables 6 and 7 show the impact of lags in project completion and attainment of full capacity for the *same* projects investigated previously, under the assumption that one-half the capital is committed at time zero. Therefore, for the reference project, with $A=3$ and $a=1$, the calculations show the economic costs of tying up capital in advance of its utilisation. At a time discount rate of 7 percent, this is about 6 percent of the capital involved in the whole project: at 15 percent, this is about 13

TABLE 6.   Project Net Worth as a Function of Project
Completion: One-Half Capital Tied

$r = 0.07$
$C = 0.10$

$k=1$; $(1\text{-}c) = 0.24$		$k=2$; $(1\text{-}c) = 0.36$		$k=3$; $(1\text{-}c) = 0.49$	
A	V	A	V	A	V
2	-0.02	2	-0.05	2	-0.09
3	-.06	3	-.13	3	-.21
4	-.10	4	-.20	4	-.32
5	-.13	5	-.27	5	-.42
6	-.17	6	-.34	6	-.51

$r = 0.15$
$C = 0.10$

$k=1$; $(1\text{-}c) = 0.34$		$k=2$; $(1\text{-}c) = 0.56$		$k=3$; $(1\text{-}c) = 0.78$	
A	V	A	V	A	V
2	-0.06	2	-0.13	2	-0.20
3	-.13	3	-.28	3	-.42
4	-.21	4	.42	4	-.63
5	-.26	5	-.52	5	-.78
6	-.31	6	-.62	6	-.93

percent of the total capital. In general, the figures demonstrate
the larger gains to be had from more rapid fruition; a one-year
reduction in project completion time saves about 4 percent of
the capital invested; a two-year reduction saves 7 percent, at
the lower discount rate. At the higher discount rate, the savings
would be approximately 8 percent and 13 percent. An acceleration of the rate of capacity utilisation by six months would
save 6 percent of the capital employed and an acceleration by
two years more than 16 percent, at a 7 percent discount factor.
At a 15 percent discount rate, these savings would be approximately the same, since the higher operating margins and higher
discount rates largely cancel each other out. If one puts these

TABLE 7. Project Net Worth as a Function of Attainment of Full Capacity Output: One-Half Capital Tied

r = 0.07
C = 0.10

$k=1$; $(1\text{-}c) = 0.24$		$k=2$; $(1\text{-}c) = 0.36$		$k=3$; $(1\text{-}c) = 0.49$	
$t{:}g(t) = 0.85$	V	$t{:}g(t) = 0.85$	V	$t{:}g(6) = 0.85$	V
1.5	-0.03	1.5	-0.08	1.5	-0.15
2.0	-.06	2.0	-.13	2.0	-.21
2.5	-.12	2.5	-.24	2.5	-.35
3.8	-.22	3.0	-.40	3.8	-.56
4.7	-.30	4.7	-.51	4.7	-.71

r = 0.15
C = 0.10

$k=1$; $(1\text{-}c) = 0.34$		$k=2$; $(1\text{-}c) = 0.56$		$k=3$; $(1\text{-}c) = 0.78$	
$t{:}g(t) = 0.85$	V	$t{:}g(t) = 0.85$	V	$t{:}g(t) = 0.85$	V
1.5	-0.10	1.5	-0.23	1.5	-0.35
2.0	-.13	2.0	-.28	2.0	-.42
2.5	-.19	2.5	-.38	2.5	-.55
3.8	-.28	3.8	-.53	3.8	-.76
4.7	-.51	4.7	-.90	4.7	-1.28

figures together, it appears that the combined effect of, say, shifting to a more economical mode of financing, accelerating completion by one year, and attaining full capacity six months earlier would save an amount equal to roughly 16 percent of investment at a 7 percent discount rate, and 27 percent of investment at a 15 percent discount rate.

All the analysis so far has been conducted in terms of the marginal project with zero present value *ex ante*. Fortunately for India, not all projects are marginal: many promise much higher rates of return. For these, of course, the savings to be had from speedier execution are considerably greater. Without repeating the previous analysis in detail, Table 8 presents the

TABLE 8. Project Net Worth as a Function of Lags: The Inframarginal Project

$r = 0.15$
$C = 0.10$

$k = 1; (1\text{-}c) = 0.43$

A	V	t: g(t) = 0.85	V
2	0.38	1.5	0.33
3	.29	2.0	.29
4	.22	2.5	.22
5	.17	3.8	.14
6	.11	4.7	-.18

impact of lags on a project offering *ex ante* an internal rate of return of 20 percent if $A=3$ and $a=1$. The assumption is made, as in Tables 4 and 5, that financing is completely on a "pay-as-you-go" basis, and a comparison with those earlier tables indicates the substantially greater savings to be had from faster execution of such inframarginal projects. Project completion one year earlier saves not 4 percent but 7 percent; completion two years earlier saves not 5 percent but 12 percent. The gains from faster utilisation are similarly increased.

The next step towards a realistic cost accounting must introduce the prospect of technological change. It has often been said in recent years that such change is largely embodied in new investments and capacity of most recent vintage. This implies that in India, where the increments to capacity have been very large relative to the original stock in many industries, the benefits of technological change should be considerable, even taking into account the probably justifiable conservatism on the part of Indian planners in adopting new and unproven technologies. If the lag between process selection and the ultimate realisation of production is long, however, the project will be more quickly overtaken by obsolescence and may even prove uncompetitive.

A good example is afforded in the nitrogenous fertiliser industry, discussed in more detail in the next chapter, in which technological change has been very rapid in the last decade. The Gorakhpur project of the Fertiliser Corporation of India was sanctioned, and discussions began with the foreign technical collaborator, in 1961. At that time, the U.N. Fertiliser Mission to India was recommending that India standardise plant sizes at about 80,000 - 90,000 metric tons of nitrogen per year. At Gorakhpur, the FCI chose a plant size of 80,000 metric tons using the partial oxidation process in the ammonia plant, since the steam reformation process was then in the pilot plant stage and had not been commercially tested. Since that time, plant sizes for new investments in India have increased to 200,000 metric tons of nitrogen and in the rest of the world to considerably larger capacities, with appreciable economies of scale. At the same time, the steam reformation process has been demonstrated to be economical both in capital costs and in operating expenses.[6] Unfortunately, because of various delaying factors, Gorakhpur was not scheduled to begin regular production until early in 1968, by which time its design was virtually obsolete. In fact, the management was even in 1966, while construction was still in progress, contemplating an investment to install the steam reformation process and to balance off capacity at higher levels. *Given* the fact that production was not begun until 1968, the costs of the long gestation period due to obsolescence can be estimated by comparison with FCI's more recent project at Durgapur, which was designed in early 1966 to come on stream in 1970. Capital costs per ton of nitrogen were estimated to be about Rs 2600 at Durgapur, compared to Rs 4100 at Gorakhpur,[7] despite the inflationary escalation that occurred

in the interim. With a construction period of two years, which
is the standard in more advanced industrial nations, new fertiliser production in 1968 would come from plants of vintage
1966, i.e., of the general design as the Durgapur and Cochin
plants. The economies in capital costs that would result if
this could be achieved, in comparison with the actual performance
at Gorakhpur and other Third Plan period fertiliser projects,
would be at least 20 percent. Of course, this industry has been
one in which technological change has been particularly rapid,
and so the example is probably a rather strong one. Nonetheless,
the composition of industrial investment in India is shifting
towards more advanced and sophisticated lines, and technological change is a salient fact with which Indian industry must
reckon.

More broadly, the longer the period over which investment
projects are stretched out before benefits are realised, the
greater the uncertainty with which planners must grapple. As
each of India's five-year plans have illustrated, it is extremely
difficult to forecast five years ahead for an economy undergoing
rapid transformation in an unstable world environment. If
uncertainty were introduced formally into Indian planning,
projects with long gestation periods would have to be discounted
rather heavily on this account. Here a distinction must be made
between long gestation periods, and *lags* in completion. The
latter throw an additional burden of adjustment on the planning
mechanism, to make adjustments in interrelated projects and
in sectoral or aggregate supply and demand to preserve balance.
Even with a substantial commitment and capability in annual
planning and plan revisions, this kind of adjustment often cannot be done thoroughly, because many projects have ancillary
investments to utilise by-products or to supply inputs, and
there are no other outlets for these ancillary capacities in the

31

short run. When such ancillary investments are considered, the costs of lags are much magnified, since a substantial additional investment is then tied up unproductively.

There are some economists who feel that these imbalances have an important and constructive role to play in economic development, because they feel that the really scarce resource in underdeveloped countries is entrepreneurial spirit and decision-making ability.[8] This premise leads to an espousal of a development strategy which maximises induced investment and development-oriented decisions by creating significant (costly) imbalances between projects, which cry out for remedy. There may be countries in which entrepreneurship rather than real resources is the constraining scarcity; certainly India is not among them. Moreover, one is led by the preceding analysis to suspect that, in view of the tremendous resource cost of such imbalances, any country which attempted to carry out such a strategy would soon encounter a resource constraint, had one not earlier been effective. In any case, given the uncertainties and the difficulties involved in maintaining balances among projects and at the aggregate level, a deliberate effort to create imbalances is unnecessary: a sufficient number would surely arise.

If such unbalanced growth strategies are suspect, the "big push" arguments at the other extreme are not therefore more credible. For the most part, these arguments for exploitation of pecuniary externalities through simultaneous investments in interrelated sectors rest on the costs of time lost in "unplanned" market recognition and capture of investment opportunities as they emerge in more sequential fashion. These costs can be substantial only if the investments which would be deferred but for "planning" promise a substantial comparative advantage: the extreme case is investment in infrastructure—

nontradable sectors like power and internal transport — which is highly inframarginal almost by definition. Potential projects within the complex which are not expected to yield a relatively large discounted return based on the alternative cost of continued imports can be deferred with little cost to the economy.

The remainder of this chapter, however, suggests that the margin of international competitiveness often stems largely from the quality of project planning, execution, and operation, which cannot be taken for granted in developing economies. For this reason, interdependencies or "linkages" may easily be *overexploited* if success, in terms of speedy completion and utilisation, becomes dependent on fine synchronisation of linked projects. It is difficult to maintain that degree of schedule control. It is especially difficult, and unqualified "big push" strategies become clearly unproductive, if budgeting of uncommitted foreign exchange or management reserves is too tight to allow enough flexibility that shortages arising from shocks to the investment plan can be made good.[9] Without this flexibility, the consistency of a development plan can be quickly lost and costly imbalances encountered. This possibility commends the concept of a core plan, which can be expanded as the resource position and the state of project preparation permits, but which contains those reserves which are justified when risk and uncertainty are admitted into the planning framework.

While contemplating questions of comparative advantage, economists have generally assumed that firms are efficient suboptimising resource allocators: minimising costs and maximising profits in the light of externally determined demand and supply conditions. Therefore, attention has centered on determinants of comparative advantage external to the firm: resource and factor endowments, national differences in tastes or consumption patterns, differential patterns of technological change, and so on. Yet, in India and probably in other developing countries as well, the assumption that even a majority of firms are efficient cost-minimisers is unrealistic. Probably the reverse is true: in most enterprises there is considerable allocative inefficiency.[10] Effective exchange rates reflect a generally low level of productivity in the use of resources for both import-competing and export production.

Moreover, in rapidly industrialising economies the supply of qualified managerial talent is limited and fairly inelastic in the short run. Nor can this talent be assumed highly mobile within the industrial sector. The close association between management and ownership, the occurrence of nepotism, and the limited interchange of management between public and private sector enterprises, all serve to restrict substantially the mobility of management personnel.

If this view of reality is acceptable, then it is possible to suppose that a firm or an industry which can be established and operated with a relatively high degree of efficiency will have an effective comparative advantage. The preceding analysis has emphasised the importance of gestation and development periods in determining the rate of return on investment and the level of costs. This suggests that enterprises with the ability to plan and implement projects successfully will probably be among the more successful in import-substitution or export production.

From another point of view, it is interesting to consider the problem faced by Indian planners in trying to determine long-run comparative advantage. Years of import controls, discriminatory export subsidies, and price and investment controls have distorted relative prices, investment decisions, and internal cost structures to such an extent that empirical study based on historical experience is hazardous. Also, India has an ample and quite diversified resource base, plus large potential internal markets, so that the number of obvious eliminations that are possible is limited. It is also true that many of the substantial industrial investments have been in closely related complexes — in chemicals, or in the mining-metals-machinery-and-engineering complex — so that all will be interdependent for markets and inputs when they come into production after gestation periods of several years. Introduce into this context the existence of significant economies of scale and "infant industry" economies of the learning curve variety, and it becomes obvious that demand factors within India, which, incidentally, enjoys considerable natural protection from its location, will have a strong influence on long-term comparative advantage. Therefore, both the level and the distribution of income are involved, as well as the rate of time discount and the planning horizon. In sum, the analytical task is formidable. Therefore, just as it is difficult to determine India's long-term advantage, so it is equally difficult to argue that any particular investment strategy, that embodied in India's Plans, for example, is nonoptimal with regard to some implicit set of parameters.

It *is* possible to contend, however, with a high degree of confidence, that within any overall investment strategy those projects which are selected without the most careful and detailed prior study and without adequate provision for management of a high calibre will very probably encounter costly delays in completion and the attainment of full capacity in efficient operation. These projects, if past experience is any guide, will be the unsuccessful import-substitutes and export producers. In other words, the range of variation in costs, from the more efficient to the less efficient, is at least as great as the variation in other dimensions more commonly associated with comparative advantage: scale, location, factor costs, and so on.

The following paragraphs attempt to illustrate this point by applying the previous analysis in conjunction with the results of several recent studies in the economics of Indian industry. One such is William Johnson's interesting study of the steel industry.[11] This study, based on estimated capital costs of a new mill and operating costs of an existing private sector mill, investigated the overall economics of expanding the Indian steel industry during the Fourth Plan period and the economics of location for a new mill at various sites proposed in India. Shadow prices were used to correct obvious distortions and approach a measure of social rate of return. The most important of these, the shadow exchange rate, has been subsequently validated by devaluation. Some of the findings most significant for the present purpose are listed below:

a) Not only are capital costs a large proportion of the industry's total costs of production, but also many other costs that are normally considered variable costs elsewhere are more properly treated as fixed costs in India. For example, most labor costs are for all practical purposes fixed in all but the very long run as a result of wage determination and restrictions on dismissals by state and central governments. . . . Rough estimates place the industry's fixed cost of production at as high as eighty or ninety percent. (page 252)

b) The present value of investment in a new steel mill is Rs. 1159 million or Rs. 2027 million, at a time discount of 10%, depending on whether a third-stage expansion to a capacity of 2.5 million tons is contemplated. This corresponds to internal rates of return of 13.2% and 14.9%. (pages 120, 121) The industry is sufficiently close to the margin that its economics cannot be taken for granted. (page 264)

c) After consideration of six alternative sites in North, East, West and South India, it was found that the *maximum* cost advantage of any mill over any other, including both production and transportation economies, would be Rs. 68 per ton of salable steel. This would accrue to a North Indian mill using North Indian coal specialised in the production of rails and heavy sections. The maximum cost advantage considering the average of three possible product mixes—rails and heavy sections, bars and light sections, and flat products—would be Rs. 42 per ton of salable steel. (page 210)

Preserving Johnson's basic data and assumptions, it is interesting to calculate the effects of the variations considered earlier in the chapter. First, assume that the new mill would be financed not on a "pay-as-you-go" basis but at least in part by a foreign credit contracted early in the project life. This has been uniformly true in the past. The USSR credit for Bokaro, construction of which had just begun in 1966, was concluded in 1963, for example. If one-half the capital—for the first stage and each expansion—were thus tied up in the first year of the investment, then the present value of investment in a 2.5 million ton mill would be reduced from Rs 2027 to Rs 1723, by Rs 354 million. At the 10 percent discount rate, this is equivalent to a difference in the annual fixed costs of Rs 32 million.

Second, assume that, with half the capital tied up, it would be possible to complete the investment one year early and thereby commence production one year earlier at each stage. This implies a telescoping of investment: Table 9 presents the assumed pattern of investment in Johnson's analysis and in this exercise. Coincidentally, this would restore the present value of the investment to Rs 2028 million, a gain of Rs 355 million equivalent again to Rs 32 million in annual fixed charges.[12]

TABLE 9. Alternative Assumptions about the Time Distribution of Investment

	Initial Stage (percent)		Subsequent Expansions (percent)	
Year	Johnson	Alternative	Johnson	Alternative
0	0.5	50 + 2.5	15	50 + 1.5
1	12	15	35	25
2	36	20	35	10
3	35	10	15	0
4	15	2.5	0	0
5	2	0	0	0

Third, assume that the value of production rises more quickly from completed capacity. In Johnson's analysis the increment to production was postulated to be 40, 80, 90, and 100 percent of the increment to capacity in each of the successive years. If utilisation were marginally accelerated to 50, 90, 100, and 100 percent of new capacity at each stage, the present value of the project would be increased by Rs 254 million, equivalent to a reduction in annual fixed costs by Rs 23 million. This marginal improvement in capacity utilisation has a relatively large effect, because fixed costs are so important. Johnson has assumed them equal to 75 percent of the total, including much of the labour force as fixed in the short run. It should be kept in mind that faster growth in the *value* of output is desirable, not an uneconomic attempt to achieve physical production norms. Johnson very forcefully and correctly stated the harmful effects overemphasis of physical targets has had on quality, product mix, and maintenance of plant.

The combined effect of faster completion and faster rise to full capacity is equivalent to a reduction of Rs 55 million in annual fixed charges. For the first stages (0.77 million tons of salable steel), this is Rs 71 per ton; for the second (1.5 million tons), it is Rs 47 per ton. The average over the first two stages is thus Rs 54 per ton. The savings that would result from a pattern of financing which did not unduly immobilise foreign capital would increase this total by Rs 31, to Rs 85 per ton. This magnitude is considerably larger than the potential economies to be realised by selecting the best possible site of the proposed alternatives instead of the worst.

Further, the steel industry has been widely criticised, along with other public-sector enterprises, for carrying an excessive labour force. Total employment in the public sector mills is about three times that which would be used in comparable plants in the West; yet the total labour costs of the average public sector mill is only Rs 80 million per year.[13] Therefore, even if it were possible to reduce the wage bill by half, the savings would be less than those generated by the reduction of gestation lags and underutilised capital and capacity.[14] In a capital-intensive industry in a country in which labour is cheap and capital is scarce, it is the rapid and full use of capital which matters most.

Another study which throws considerable light on the question is the intriguing investigation of optimal patterns of size, location, and time-phasing of investment carried out by Alan Manne and his collaborators.[15] In their simplest model, with no foreign trade and a single producing centre, the interaction of economies of scale and arithmetic growth rates of demand determine optimal plant size. Economies of scale are balanced against the costs of excess capacity resulting from expansion ahead of demand: the larger the plant, the slower the attainment of full capacity. In a more complicated model which contemplates temporary imports to meet demand until internal market growth is sufficient to justify investment, economies of scale are balanced against excess capacity and the relatively higher costs of imports. In a third model allowing multiple producing centres and inter-regional shipments, transportation costs act in the same way as do import costs.

The significant finding from the point of view of the present study is not the determination of optimal plant sizes but rather that *it makes remarkably little difference, within the assumptions of the model, what plant sizes are chosen.* The costs of under-utilised capacity obliterate the economies of scale. Therefore, plants one-half or twice optimal size appear only marginally less economical: with small plants, capital costs are high but there is little building ahead of demand; with large plants, the opposite is true. The introduction of temporary imports does not at all alter this conclusion, although the entire cost schedule is shifted downwards. If imports are very expensive, the temporary import phase is short; if they are fairly inexpensive, the temporary import phase is long. But, in either case, the amount by which domestic capacity is built ahead of demand is almost constant; therefore, overall costs are still equally insensitive to large relative deviations from the optimal size. However, in industries in which capital costs are high, or import costs are low, the penalties of deviation from optimal size over an *absolute* range of plant sizes are lower.

The fullest demonstration of this phenomenon is presented in the tables generated by Donald Erlenkotter,[16] which consider a wide range of economies of scale, time discount rates, capital intensities, and import costs. The greatest relative increase in costs from a twofold deviation from optimal plant size is there shown to be 10 percent of the total costs which vary in the model, and the median increase is between 6 and 7 percent. However, the costs which vary in the model are only the capital costs and the *difference* between import costs and the proportional operating costs of internal production (and transportation costs, in some cases). These typically represent only one-half or less of the total costs. Therefore, on the average, to build plants one-half or twice the optimal size involves a penalty of only 3 to 4 percent of total costs, given the assumptions of the model. These magnitudes, compared to the savings that would result from better time-phasing in the execution of investment projects, are surprisingly small.

This conclusion, which minimises the importance of economies of scale in project selection, stems largely from the assumption that all underutilisation of capacity is due to limitations on market size and from the assumption that demand grows at a constant arithmetic rate. In fact, the growth of demand for the outputs of many projects is quite lumpy: projects are linked in complexes and the completion of a user project will result in a spurt in demand for the supplying project's output. Moreover, most of the excess capacity that has existed in Indian industry has been unplanned, the result of mistaken forecasts of demand growth, technical difficulties, shortages of power or critical inputs, and so on. The result has been a continuation of "temporary" imports much longer than planned. Therefore, the scope for better and faster utilisation of capital is much larger than implied in these models.

Among the several valuable industry studies in the volume, it will be instructive to look more carefully at that of the nitrogenous fertiliser industry, which is the subject of the following chapter. In an elaborate and advanced investigation of possible patterns of production and transportation, encompassing (*a*) self-sufficiency within every individual state, (*b*) regional self-sufficiency with production located at single points within the region, (*c*) regional self-sufficiency with production increases

TABLE 10. Adjustment of Cost Estimates for Exchange Rate Change

Cost Item	Computed optimal programme: production costs		Worst solution costs: state self-sufficiency	
	Original	Adjusted	Original	Adjusted
Capital	222	277	313	391
Operating	407	450	407	450
Transport	40	40	28	28
Total	669	767	748	869

phased between individual states, and (d) even more complicated patterns, Manne found a best solution which reduced the discounted costs per ton of nitrogen by about Rs 80 per ton, under the costs of producing nitrogen on the basis of self-sufficiency in the individual states. [17] The total discounted cost of production in the latter case was estimated at Rs 748 per ton, implying a savings of about 11 percent. Unfortunately, this calculation was performed at the pre-devaluation exchange rate of Rs 4.75 per dollar. However, it is possible to make approximate adjustments: the imported component of capital costs is no more than 50 percent and will in the future be closer to 30 percent; since naphtha is treated as a surplus by-product in India, as the major element in operating costs, it should be little affected by a change in the exchange rate; also, the immediate effect on transportation costs should be small. Table 10 presents the worst and best solutions in Manne's calculations, showing the components of capital, transport, and operating costs in the solution. It also shows the adjustment based on a 50 percent revaluation of the exchange rate, an assumed 50 percent foreign component in capital costs, and an *ad hoc* increase in operating costs. Therefore, at an adjusted exchange rate, the savings appear to be still about 11 or 12 percent, or about Rs 100 per ton.

Fertiliser production, given current world prices, appears strongly inframarginal in India. At the new exchange rate, the CIF price of nitrogen in the form of urea was about Rs 1850 per ton in 1966. [18] However, the trend of nitrogenous fertiliser prices has been markedly downwards in recent years, due to technological improvements and excess capacity. The relevant opportunity cost for India, still largely dependent on imports, is probably Rs 1000 per ton of nitrogen, which corresponds to a CIF price of $60 per ton of urea. For comparative purposes, it is interesting to calculate the potential savings from a reduction in gestation times. Preserving Manne's data, the parameters of the model would be as follows:

$$k = \frac{1.2875 \times 175 \times 10^6 \ (X/77.5)^{.73}}{1000 \times 10^3 \ (X)} = 2.25 \text{ for a plant size of 200,000 tons of } N$$

$(p - c) / p = (1000 - 450) / 1000 = 0.55$

$(C/X) / p = 140/1000 = 0.14$

$r \qquad = 0.10$

$L \qquad = 15$

$A \qquad = 2.5 \text{ or } 3.5$

$a \qquad = 1.25 \text{ or } 1.00$

With these parameters, the present value of a nitrogenous fertiliser factory which would go into production after two and a half years and reach 90 percent of rated capacity output within two more years would be about three-tenths of a year's output, corresponding to an internal rate of approximately 14 percent. In other words, with substantially lower world prices to be expected, fertiliser production in India appears mildly inframarginal.

Nonetheless, if the start of production from a new large plant were delayed by a single year, even on the assumption that no part of the capital requirement is committed until actually expended, and if after two years only 85 percent of full capacity output were attained rather than 90 percent, then the present value of the loss would be Rs 130 per ton of output. Since this estimate is in terms of present value, it is directly comparable to the estimated savings of Rs 100 per ton which would stem from a choice of the best pattern of scales, locations, and time-phasings instead of the worst. This result underscores the point that, for inframarginal projects, the savings from accelerated realisation of benefits are of primary importance.

In rapidly industrialising economies, it has long been recognised that managerial and administrative capacity is scarce. The comparisons just presented illustrate the value of successful management, a difference in investment returns of at least the same magnitude as those due to locational factors, economies of scale, labour costs, and so on. Yet, in project study, the question of management is usually the last to be considered; on the abstract level of international trade theory it is considered hardly at all. In countries like India, in which competitive forces to cull out the inefficient have been limited and in which the long-range options for development strategy are numerous, management's ability to carry out the detailed planning and implementation of investment projects and to bring them quickly up to full productivity will often determine success or failure in meeting international competition.

3 The Pace of Infant Industry Economies: A Study of the Fertiliser Corporation of India

Taking the results of the last chapter as a point of departure, the following pages explore the hypothesis that important infant industry economies may result from experience and increased competence in the planning and implementation of investment projects. As Harry Johnson has put it, the nature of infant industry conditions is "an empirical issue concerning which the ratio of unsupported assertion to empirical evidence is probably unexcelled in any other field of economics."[1] Since policy arguments based on the existence of external economies are so frequently encountered in development planning, it is important to investigate the nature and sources of such economies, and more importantly, to know what policies and organisational arrangements will ensure their realisation. The preceding chapter suggests that a learning curve in the broad area of project planning and management would probably be quantitatively significant in its effects on investment returns. Also, since a project is by nature a discrete event, so that anything learned from project experience cannot be internalised but must be applied to subsequent projects, such economies are likely to be really external to the individual undertaking.

Exploration of the learning process in investment activities is particularly relevant to the issues raised by a number of recent policy-oriented studies emphasising absorptive capacity as a limiting factor to the transfer of capital and the pace of development.[2] These studies begin with the commonsense observation that, so long as the marginal efficiency of capital exceeds its cost to the developing economy, the growth of income with a fixed supply of capital to be allocated over time will be maximised, or the total input of capital over time to achieve a given growth of income will be minimised, by supplying the additional capital as early in time as possible. These studies then assert that the amount of capital transfer possible in any period is limited by sharply declining marginal efficiency of investment or by absolute limits on the amount of investment possible in any period, an expression of limited absorptive capacity. This formulation leads naturally to relatively pessimistic conclusions about the attainable rate of growth in poor countries and the amount of capital assistance rich countries can usefully provide.

The assumption of severe limits on the ability of poor countries to invest evidently stems less from any extensive knowledge of the limiting factors than from the common spectacle in past years of lending agencies searching vainly around the world for projects suitable and ready for financial support. Implicitly, the model assumes the existence of some input into the investment process in extremely inelastic supply: management, technicians, construction workers, or perhaps some entrepreneurial ability. It follows that in the model the implicit rent or shadow price on this limiting factor is extremely high. It also follows in reality that, insofar as full utilisation of available domestic or foreign savings is limited, or the costs of investment sharply increased, by bottlenecks in the investment process, the potential payoff to actions which eliminate such bottlenecks will be enormous. Further, the higher the implicit rate of time discount, the greater this payoff will be. These considerations also support the notion that a learning process in project planning and management may be of considerable significance.

On closer examination the assumption of some input in inelastic supply limiting investment activity becomes less plausible. Just as virtually every capital good or material input into capital formation is importable, so virtually every human and intangible input is also importable. After all, broad and specialised economic, industrial, and engineering consultants are easily obtainable; technical knowledge can be had under license or other arrangements; competent contracting firms are available to assume full responsibility for construction, erection, and commissioning, or any portion thereof. Even operating management can be imported under contract or obtained through foreign private investment. The appropriate model for the analysis of investment activity is a model of import substitution. The rational decisions for developing countries are "make-or-buy" decisions, in which the payoffs to relaxation of the "constraint" on absorptive capacity by importing skills are balanced against the long-run benefits of developing indigenous skills and experience in managing investment projects. As with import substitution in other sectors, the higher the rate of time discount, the more favourable will appear the option to import. Similarly, the policy issues facing lending agencies revolve around the means to break constraints in absorptive capacity by providing technical assistance, or resources and encouragement for the poorer countries to import such skills independently, or by assisting in the development of indigenous capabilities. Given the high implicit rent on ivestment ability, programmes of this nature would tend to yield high returns.

To illuminate some of the elements involved in the development of indigenous investment ability, the Fertiliser Corporation of India was chosen as a significant subject for study. FCI is a large, multiplant public-sector firm which in 1966 contributed more than half the total ouput of the Indian nitrogenous fertiliser industry. It, or its organisational predecessors, had up to 1967 participated in eight major new projects, as well as several substantial expansions. The general directive governing FCI's current expansion plans was to be prepared to undertake two new projects during the Fourth Plan period in addition to those underway at the end of the Third Plan period. In some of their past projects, they had experienced serious difficulties and long delays in the completion of work, so their growing capacity to carry out their heavy responsibilities has been a matter of considerable interest. Indeed, during the Third Plan period, large shortfalls in fertiliser production had serious consequences. As against the initial target for capacity of one million tons of N, and the midterm revision of 800,000, capacity at the end of 1965 - 1966 had reached roughly 500,000 tons and production was scarcely 300,000. The shortage of fertilisers in the middle years of the plan undoubtedly contributed to agricultural shortfalls and slowed the rate of adoption, while compensating imports involved a heavy foreign exchange outlay in addition to the sums tied up in the expansion program. In the Fourth Plan, capacity in the industry was expected to quadruple and production to increase five-fold. Slippages in this program would have serious consequences. Also, the sheer magnitude of the proposed investment in fertiliser, estimated to be approximately Rs 400 crores just for Fourth Plan increases in the industry, emphasises the importance of productive use of this capital.

This study relies heavily on four months of interviews with senior and middle management of the various divisions of FCI, supplemented by an examination of internal documents and public reports.[3] Primary attention was given to three successive projects: Nangal (1955 - 1961), Gorakhpur (1961 - 1967), and Durgapur (1966 -) to see what were the problems encountered in the earlier projects leading to long gestation periods, how they were recognised and countered by management and government, and to what improvements in subsequent performance these adaptations led.

The problems the Fertiliser Corporation of India has faced are, in fact, very much like those encountered in other Indian industries both public and, to an extent, private. To substantiate this in detail would be too time-consuming, but there exist enough case studies and evaluation reports to do so.[4] A general sketch of the most critical problem areas, however, may be helpful:

1. Projects, especially in the public sector, have been consistently delayed by the prolonged process of decision-making regarding essential features of the undertaking, such as size, location, process, output mix, mode of implementation, and financing. Often, even in priority projects, this process has taken longer than actual implementation. The reasons are many. One is the instability of the economic environment, including conditions surrounding foreign credits, and the uncertainty regarding the state of the market after three to six years, when the project would come on stream. Some of this is inherent in an economy undergoing rapid structural change. Some of it is due to tight resource constraints managed by rigid direct controls, which tend to result in supply inelasticities and volatile price relations and to obscure real demand patterns.[5] In fact, long gestation periods increase the forecasting problem, to which the conscientious reaction is further study to refine the data available for decision, which further lengthens the gestation period. In certain projects in the past, this cycle of redefinition and restudy threatened to continue indefinitely.

Another problem has been the diffusion of responsibility for project-planning and decision, and the extensive provisions for review which have prevailed. This has been largely an attempt to ensure conformity of the individual project with overall financial and sectoral plans and policies, in the context of rapid structural change. It has also been, in the public sector, a reflection of some lack of confidence in the capabilities of management in the enterprises to plan and define new projects, when, in fact, management in some enterprises lacked the experience and staff to do so. It has been, in the private sector, a reflection of government's lack of confidence in market signals and the price mechanism, when, in fact, relative prices have been both volatile and distorted. The result, however, has been a time-consuming process of deliberation, clarification, revision, and review by a multitude of agencies.

2. A related problem has been frequent revision of project plans after execution has begun, entailing considerable loss of time. Sometimes, new conditions or information have arisen to enforce changes in plans. Sometimes, however, inadequacies in planning have been at fault. These not only have delayed decision-making, as sketchy planning work was clarified and amplified in the review process, but also have led to regrettable and costly changes later on. Also, inadequate attention to the cost of time has sometimes permitted changes in scope where not absolutely necessary, in order to effect marginal cost economies or to meet additional demands, at a price in lost time which would be found to outweigh the real benefits to be gained.

3. A third problem has been delay in procurement, encompassing land acquisition, contract award and approval, import licensing and foreign exchange release, and procurement of scarce domestic materials. Land acquisition, especially if many owners or tenants occupy the desired site, has frequently been a protracted process of negotiation of adequate compensation, appeal through the courts, agitation and local political skirmishing, and problems of resettling the "oustees." These problems touch complex legal and social issues.

Numerous difficulties have similarly hampered the letting of contracts: accumulation of data needed for the preparation of tender invitations, which often rest on submissions by design consultants or equipment suppliers; evaluation of bids when the invitations to tender permit wide divergence among bidders in scope, design, foreign exchange component, and so on; sometimes, problems of finding qualified bidders within the country for domestic services, or in the country of origin for country-tied aid-financed projects; problems of negotiation when, for one reason or another, there is less than adequate competition among bidders; problems of fixing responsibility narrowly enough to avoid time-consuming review or committee deliberations. The result of all these problems has been that delays, sometimes as long as a year or more, have not infrequently occurred in the finalisation of key contracts, retarding progress on the whole project.

Procurement problems associated with import licensing have so many ramifications and strike so deeply that the subject requires a book to itself. Basically, however, the extreme balance of payments constraint has engendered a system of import control involving close scrutiny of proposed foreign exchange expenditure for essentiality and domestic availability of equivalent items, a complicated problem of matching import demands against various tied foreign exchange sources, and heavy competition and long queues for extremely limited amounts of free foreign exchange. This has been the Indian situation for over a decade, during which time, despite repeated efforts to "streamline" procedures, delays in obtaining critical import items have disrupted schedules, delayed completion of projects by months, and interfered with full production from new facilities once complete. Similarly, shortages and rationing of domestic materials in short supply at one time or another, including iron and steel, cement, coal and coke, nonferrous metals, and rail transport, have interfered with timely procurement.

4. A fourth problem has been inadequate control over schedule in both pre-construction and construction phases of new projects. In relatively new industries, the development of realistic operating schedules has been hampered by the lack of sufficient data on the resources and time required under Indian conditions to complete various project activities. The lack of detailed and meticulous project planning at an early stage has also been at times a handicap to schedule development.

These scheduling deficiencies have contributed to an excessively loose control over contractor performance, i.e., control not based on well-defined contractual responsibilities to meet definite and detailed schedule commitments. This has been a particularly serious problem in Indian industry, since few highly qualified contracting firms exist for many kinds of fabrication, construction, and erection work. Frequently, contracting firms are deficient in equipment, technical and supervisory personnel, highly skilled labour, and trained management. Therefore, successful project execution in India often requires a more intensive supervision of contractor performance and adoption by project management of many planning responsibilities that in other countries might be delegated in large part to the contractor.

5. A fifth problem has been lack of synchronisation in interdependent projects, leading to delays in the availability of inputs or in the emergence of markets. When slippages in infrastructure, like power or transport, have occurred, these have been particularly damaging, since compensating imports are impossible; but, even for other inputs, foreign exchange constraints have sometimes delayed or prohibited compensating imports as well. Slippages in forward-linked projects have delayed full utilisation of new capacity, since alternative uses or export markets

can rarely be found within a short period. This problem returns full circle to the difficulties involved in "consistent" planning of interrelated projects in a rapidly changing environment without full control of all schedules.

With this introduction, it is now possible to explore specific adaptations by which the Fertiliser Corporation of India has countered such problems in the field of project management. It must be emphasised that the process of learning and adaptation is by no means complete. On the contrary, several examples are given below of economies and benefits yet to be realised.

One specific adaptation lies in the area of industrial organisation, and concerns the formation of the FCI itself. This step was a conscious attempt to capture infant industry economies by internalising them. The government of India has by-and-large favoured the unification of projects into large multiplant organisations rather than the proliferation of separate undertakings. Thus, in 1961, with the acceptance of new projects at Namrup and Gorakhpur, the original Sindri Fertilisers & Chemicals Ltd. and the Hindustan Chemicals & Fertilisers Ltd. , which had responsibility for plants at Nangal and Trombay, were merged to form the FCI. FCI now has responsibility for most of the expansion program in the public sector. Past exceptions to this principle of unification are Rourkela and Neyveli, which form parts of distinct industrial complexes, and FACT in Kerala, which has a long career of its own.

It is worth quoting from the influential report of the Fertiliser Production Committee (1956) to convey some of the thinking behind this policy:

In considering what would be the best mode of carrying out the approved projects, we have been impressed by the need for and importance of pooling and centralising the technical and administrative resources that will be at Government's command. ... Much of the potentiality of State-owned fertiliser projects will be lost if they are regarded in future as separate entities, and each is managed by a different Board and allowed to develop its own standards and traditions with only a loose type of coordination at the level of the Ministry . . . [It is] , in our considered view, essential that all of them, old and new, should be fully integrated and administered as a well-knit joint endeavour under common direction and control . . .

The unification of control which we visualize will not only ensure quick and coordinated planning and execution of all projects . . . and expeditious investigation and solution of all engineering problems, but also render possible the establishment of centralised fabrication facilities, a central drawing and design office, a central research and development bureau, ... a central marketing office, etc. ... Further, the constitution of a central authority controlling all State-owned fertiliser production units will facilitate all-round practical training of technical personnel in various types of plants and processes, and free exchange of personnel between different units to ensure that the right man is available for the job at the right time.[6]

What the committee was urging, in effect, was a policy designed to internalise the external economies of industrial development by freeing the exchange of information and personnel and by overcoming indivisibilities in the production of various planning and research services.

This policy has yielded demonstrable benefits. Under it, for example, the FCI has generated a fully staffed and equipped planning, design, and research division at Sindri, with specialised teams for process design, engineering, fundamental research, and also for techno-economic studies relevant to the industry in general or to particular projects. As this division has grown, it has gradually substituted local for imported services in project planning, design and engineering, and project management. In contrast to the first fertiliser project at Sindri, which was implemented after independence under two main contracts, one with a firm of consulting engineers, the other with a "constructor" who selected contractors and coordinated and supervised their work, the owner's responsibilities in Third Plan projects like Gorakhpur included management of civil works and erection, as well as complete responsibility for most ancillary facilities. In its most recent projects like that at Durgapur, FCI is acting practically as its own "turnkey" contractor. Apart from certain process know-how and design services provided by the foreign technical collaborator (FACT is also providing certain engineering services on contract to FCI, by virtue of its purchase of some of the relevant process know-how), complete responsibility for all phases of the project lies directly with FCI. This has important implications for design, procurement, contracting, and control of schedule. What is important to recognise is that this development could not have taken place without the pooling of available talent and know-how in a single organisation and a sufficient scale of operations and expansions to justify such an establishment. These, in turn, stem directly from the decision to integrate public sector fertiliser units under the FCI. In this instance, therefore, the position of the "learning curve" has depended on a change in industrial organisation.[7]

In the future, further economies may result from other organisational changes. For example, the present mode of cooperation between FCI and FACT, which will evidently share the bulk of future public-sector expansions, is cumbersome. The two organisations are now sharing purchased process know-how and each contributing engineering services to the other's project. This introduces two more agencies into the project organisation and raises additional problems of coordination. Also, the logic of FCI's growth suggests that specialised construction and erection management teams be formed and located organisationally as part of a "projects division" distinct from operating divisions. At present, a site organisation is set up when a project is approved for execution, with certain functions to perform during the project stage. It later becomes the operating division. While it and the Planning and Development Division have common objectives and naturally try to work in close cooperation, experience has already shown that this division creates problems of day-to-day communication and coordination. Integration of all project activities within one group would promote the closest possible coordination and also the development of specialised experience and expertise in construction and erection management.[8]

The implications of the import substitution in project services which has accompanied the growth of the Planning and Development Division shed light on the benefits of the learning experience. First of all, with greater local engineering, it has been possible to seek more actively for ways to increase the Indian component of plant and equipment. FCI engineers have surveyed local fabrication capabilities and have actively collaborated with potential suppliers. In some instances, it has been possible to modify the specifications of materials, vessels, or equipment to bring them into consonance with suppliers' capabilities, with no repercussions on the overall process design. This is something foreign engineers could do as well, but there is little incentive for them to undertake the extra effort, or to depart from their conventional engineering standards and specifications, and it is difficult to force them to do so, especially if performance guarantees are demanded. One indication of the extent to which Indian efforts have been successful is the increase in the local content of plant and equipment from 10 to 20 percent in the foreign-engineered plants at Trombay and Gorakhpur to 40 to 50 percent in the Indian-engineered plants at Durgapur and Cochin.[9]

Secondly, local design has facilitated modifications to bring international designs into closer accord with Indian conditions. In India, for example, maintenance tends to be a relatively more serious problem, in part because of the lack of experience of operating personnel, in part because of the time-consuming procedures for obtaining replacements, mostly from abroad out of free foreign exchange. Yet, the increasing sophistication and competition of the chemical engineering business has led to plant designs ever more closely restricted to rated capacity, with less built-in spare capacity, so that it has become more difficult to attain and sustain this rated level of output.[10] Indian engineers have tended to be on the conservative side, in building in a margin of safety and avoiding unproven or hairline designs. This may be a more economical course under Indian conditions.[11]

Another advantage of the trend toward wholly indigenous engineering is its impact on schedule. In the past, FCI has experienced considerable difficulty in obtaining a timely flow of data and drawings, and this has led to interruptions in the orderly progress of contracting, engineering, fabrication, civil works, and erection. When, in addition to the owner, there are separate contractors, many of them foreign, for civil works, civil engineering, plant design and engineering and equipment supply, with numerous subcontractors for fabrication, the lines of communication tend to become excessively complicated. Effective coordination is difficult. Moreover, the schedule most to the advantage of the owner may imply a sequence of work which does not minimise cost to some or any of the contractors. Then, real problems arise in holding contractors to schedule

commitments.[12]   A unified engineering responsibility, like
that evolved by the FCI acting as its own "turnkey" contractor,
ameliorates many of these problems. Communications are
improved, and conflicts of interest are reduced. As a result,
time lost through interruption in the even flow of work has
been reduced.

A more significant benefit that has resulted from import
substitution in design and engineering is the degree of standardisation it has permitted. Standardisation of plant and equipment
design in the past has been difficult to achieve, because financing
has linked procurement to particular countries and because
foreign engineering firms, with their own engineering practices
and standards and holding only certain licenses for process
know-how, have been entrusted with the job. Recently, however,
the interaction of local design and greater reliance on foreign
suppliers' credits (to be discussed below) has permitted FCI to
plan at least four major projects — Durgapur and Cochin, Barauni
and Namrup Extension — which will be very similar.

One result of standardisation will be a reduction of difficulties and delay in contracting. Technical information will be
available at a very early date to permit the contracting process
to begin. Of greater significance is the prospect of significant
reductions in project time schedules as well as costs. Design
and engineering time on subsequent plants should be reduced
by several months. Quoted delivery times for critical equipment
should be shortened by a few months, not only because of the
learning curve in fabricators' shops but also because of the
reduction in contingency margins usually included in the suppliers' quotations when substantial penalties for late delivery
are imposed in contract terms. Erection and commissioning
time, and the time required to stabilise production at high
levels, may also be reduced, but this will depend largely on the

extent to which key personnel experienced in previous plants of the same design are included in the erection and commissioning teams. Even larger benefits from standardisation would be possible were bulk orders or long-term supply contracts placed for critical equipment and materials, which would permit real production economies and reduce delivery lead times as well. To do this for imported equipment, in advance of firm financing commitments, would involve a measure of risk, but this risk could be reduced by taking options on delivery of equipment critical to the schedule, and the result might be a significant overall reduction in completion time.

In addition to these time savings, standardisation will lead to cost savings of perhaps 5 percent of total capital costs in subsequent projects, due to 40 to 50 percent reduction in design and engineering costs; reduced payments to the foreign collaborators for checking of drawings; supervision of erection and use of licensed know-how; reduced spares and inventories; and reduced indigenous procurement costs due to economies of scale and reduced wastage of materials. Indian chemical plant producers, operating with considerable unutilised capacity, will be able to pass along the advantages of longer production runs and a reduction in the number of items manufactured.[13]

Another critical area in which the benefits of experience have been apparent is that of project planning. Not only in the FCI, nor only in the fertiliser industry, nor only in India, deficiencies in investment planning have been a serious source of cost and schedule overruns.[14] It is evident, however, from an examination of the project plans on which decisions and actions have been taken that the FCI has made considerable progress in generating thorough and competent project studies. For early projects, the basic techno-economic studies which usually underlay project approval were carried out by foreign consultants, *ad hoc* committees of Indian experts, or by the engineering departments of operating divisions.[15] Examination of these studies for earlier projects like Nangal and Gorakhpur reveals serious limitations on the quality of relevant data available at the time of decision, the adequacy of economic analysis, and the amount of detailed technical and administrative planning accomplished at an early stage, in comparison to the plans for later projects like that at Durgapur. More recently, a single department within the Planning and Development Division has been formed to make continuing studies of demand, location and design of new units; and raw materials and equipment availability, as well as techno-economic studies for particular projects under consideration. This has obvious advantages: the accumulation of expertise and experience; the possibility of engaging in long-term and continuing studies of the basic economic and technical factors affecting the industry; and the creation of a central repository for relevant price, cost, and process information. Moreover, it fixes responsibility for the execution of these functions in a single agency, operating under policy guidelines from above, instead of having responsibility diffused throughout the organisation and various organs of government.

Naturally, the upgrading of investment planning is a continuing process. A significant area of development for the future will be additional steps to integrate planning at various levels: that of the project, the industry, the sector, and the economy. At present, despite the existence of Five Year Plans, much of this is done at the level of the ministry through a time-consuming process of discussion and review of project plans, and considerable attention has been given to ways of simplifying procedures.[16] Part of the problem seems to be a shortage of useful policy guidelines and operational planning criteria, based on broader sectoral and economic studies, under which many of the detailed suboptimisation decisions of detailed project planning could be safely left to the individual enterprise. The clearest of such criteria, of course, is the explicit trade-off or "price" defining the relative cost of alternatives. One aspect of the problem, therefore, has been the degree to which actual market prices have failed to reflect, even to the government's satisfaction, actual relative resource costs. In the absence of these useful criteria, the only alternative to unconditional delegation of planning responsibility has been review of individual decisions on "merit." For the public sector, development of more efficient means of linking planning at various levels and permitting decentralisation without loss of control will contribute to the reduction of time spent in the review and revision of project plans. For the private sector, in which any attempt to monitor investment plans in all but the largest projects has proven clearly beyond administrative capabilities, the only pressure that government can apply to improve the quality of investment planning is market pressure, by ensuring that market prices reflect the true costs of time, foreign exchange, and other scarce factors, and by ensuring that firms are subject to sufficient competition to spur increases in efficiency. Clearly, the pace of the learning process is influenced strongly by the amount of pressure on the enterprise to reduce costs and raise productivity.

The previous chapter emphasised the important role the length of the gestation period has in determining project costs and profitability. Consequently, a most significant area in which experience has led to economies is that of project scheduling, reporting, and control. Since so many concurrent and interrelated activities take place, executed by so many agencies, in a major investment project, the detailed analysis and scheduling of work is fundamental to fix the responsibilities of all parties and to direct efforts and resources into a consistent pattern. In earlier FCI projects, schedule slippage was a major problem and led to unduly long periods of time required for completion: more than five years on the average. Obviously, this imposed a considerable cost on the economy, because of the amount of capital locked into fertiliser projects and the high price of fertiliser on international markets. With Durgapur project, however, an attempt has been made from the very outset to make full use of modern techniques of scheduling and control. Both the Project Coordination Department, specially formed in the Planning and Development Division for this purpose, and the Project Planning Office at the site, have taken vigorous action to install usable systems based on network analysis, encompassing the derivation of adequate contractual milestones, procurement planning, work scheduling, management reporting, cost accounting, and data storage and analysis. This system has helped to reduce delays in the execution of the Durgapur project and will undoubtedly be of even greater service in the future as it is perfected and extended. For example, it would be highly productive if the system were extended backwards in time and applied to the numerous critical activities in the pre-construction phase of projects: land acquisition, the conclusion of agreements with suppliers and financial sources, governmental clearances, and so on. Numerous lengthy delays tend to occur in this phase, and explicit scheduling of these activities will help to pinpoint responsibility, enforce agreement among responsible agencies, and point up the consequences and costs of delay.[17]

In the area of contracting policy and procedures, experience has led the FCI toward solutions of several problems: how to avoid protracted discussion, clarification, re-tender, negotiation and review in concluding important contracts; how to ensure the selection of contractors able and equipped to perform satisfactorily; and how to gain and maintain effective control of contractor performance over the course of work. In the past, the period of contract award has been unduly extended for a number of reasons. Imprecise, overly general tender specifications or specifications which had subsequently to be revised often led to numerous requests for clarification of bids, difficulties in comparing bids submitted on widely different bases, protracted negotiations, or the solicitation of fresh bids. Over time, however, the period required for the preparation and evaluation of tenders has tended to decline, owing to FCI's increasing experience in design and engineering. In the most recent projects, process, equipment, and the scope of supply have been more closely specified in tender documents and removed from the area of negotiation, so that FCI has found itself less often faced with widely disparate bids.

Another timesaving adaptation has been to reduce the number of persons involved in bid evaluation. Evidently, during the Third Plan period, the tendency was to assemble "high-powered committees" for important contract decisions, including not only senior officers from FCI divisions but also outside experts. This undoubtedly engaged the most experienced judgements available, lent weight to the recommendations, and fostered a broad collective responsiblity for decisions, Unfortunately, however, the most senior men tended naturally to be those with the most numerous and pressing commitments elsewhere, so that it was often a task of considerable magnitude to convene them quickly enough to reach a speedy decision.[18] This tendency seems now to have been reversed, the Planning and Development Division and the site organisation sharing the major responsibilities for contracting. Similarly, a good deal of time was consumed in government in the review and approval of contracts exceeding $0.53 million, or Rs 40 lakhs (one lakh equals 100,000). Recently, an attempt has been made to shorten this process by forming a single committee comprising officers of all concerned agencies to consider such matters at one sitting.

Procedures have also been evolved to ensure the selection of qualified contractors. To give adequate weight to competence, quality, and reliability in the evaluation of bids in public-sector enterprises is difficult, because of a well-developed system of financial post-audit and a well-developed fear of venality and favouritism. Thus, a low bid, even an unrealistically low bid, cannot be rejected without elaborate justification, and even then the door is opened to complaints from dissatisfied bidders about favouritism, failure to encourage new entrants into the field, and so on. In recent projects, FCI has used a screening procedure, whereby prospective bidders are invited to submit particulars of their experience and qualifications, and tenders are invited only from those judged, with concurrence at high levels, to be eligible. For fabrication and equipment supply contracts, FCI has for reference a thorough survey of capacities and capabilities performed at periodic intervals, so that tenders can be invited only from qualified manufacturers.

Over time, this system will undoubtedly be further developed. Up until now, evaluation of contractor performance has been somewhat haphazard. Since successful performance by one contractor is highly dependent on other contractors and agencies meeting their commitments, a reliable evaluation presupposes a thorough analysis of project experience on completion. Systematic retrieval and analysis of information on project experience has just begun. In the past, most was stored in the minds of the officers concerned, and much emphasis was therefore placed on having experienced people in command. There was no group in any project organisation specifically charged with the function of collecting in a useful form potentially valuable information, and "line" officers would naturally have little time to spare for this. Moreover, there appears to have been a rather defensive attitude on the part of project executives, which led them to shy away from candid written evaluations of project experience for fear of possible future criticism.[19] This can undoubtedly be attributed to that notion of "accountability" in public-sector enterprises which encourages, even prescribes, widespread second-guessing on matters of executive judgement by auditors, ministerial civil servants, parliamentary committees of enquiry, and so on. By nature, such review is almost always done be individuals with less knowledge of the field or the particular circumstances of the case than the man who made the original decision, and its value is probably less than the costs of inhibited decision-making and inhibited evaluation of project experience which it engenders.

Other changes in contracting policy have increased FCI's ability to control contractor performance while work is in progress, primarily by building in more detailed schedules and milestones into contract documents along with provisions that give the owner adequate powers to ensure compliance. In early projects, clauses governing schedule obligations tended to be too vague to ensure effective coordination at the operational level. In more recent projects, schedule development has been advanced sufficiently early to permit the inclusion of adequate milestones in contractual agreements.

Procurement problems have been among the most troublesome of those facing investment projects in both public and private sectors. Delays in import licensing have been widespread;[20] so, to an extent, have been delays in procurement of controlled domestic items. FCI's experience has helped it to adapt to these difficult circumstances. By developing its own knowledge of Indian supply sources and consulting in advance with the government screening agency, it has been able to pre-screen its own import demands and to avoid much subsequent questioning and the need for prolonged justification. It has also taken over procurement responsibility for scarce domestic materials, in order to place indents, if necessary, in advance of contract awards for civil works or fabrication. The more important adaptations, however, have stemmed from changes in government policy. Most significantly, steps have been taken to assure sufficient foreign exchange for critical replacement and spare parts, materials, and the like. Devaluation and the liberalisation of import licensing begun in 1966 were measures designed to take some of the pressure off the licensing mechanism and to permit an easier flow of imports into priority sectors.

Discussion of such policy changes, important though they be, would move this study far afield and really outside its scope. Certain government policies, however, have been so important in establishing the environment for investment, and there are so many points of contact between project and government, that consideration of some aspects is inescapable. One of these is the complex of policies surrounding the financing of fertiliser projects. During the Third Plan period, most financing of public sector projects was under government-to-government credits. Considerable delays were experienced because of uncertainties and shifts in "aid" availability, drawn-out discussions with creditor agencies, and difficult negotiations with suppliers under these tied credits. It was, in general, the Indian experience that in projects so financed it was relatively difficult to promote standardisation and maximum use of domestic inputs and to obtain competitive price quotations when sources of supply were limited to a single country under a prearranged credit, or even, at times, to a single source within a country.[21] Moreover, the credit terms offered by some "aid-giving" agencies were not particularly favourable, relative to those available otherwise.

It was also the Third Plan experience that the pace of private investment in the fertiliser industry, and the interest displayed by potential foreign private participants, lagged behind. To private investors, the prospective returns in the industry seemed low and the investment "climate" difficult;[22] to the Indian side, foreign private capital appeared costly in terms of the returns and conditions sought by prospective investors and not particularly effective in tapping sources of foreign exchange not available to the public sector.[23] The response to this situation seems to have been two rather important shifts in emphasis in government policy. The object of one was to embolden and encourage foreign private participation. In the latter part of 1965 government policy was redefined and clarified in an effort to make such participation more attractive.[24] The response, however, in the private sector, was slow.

The other important shift in policy was a determination in 1966 to go ahead with a vigourous expansion program in the public sector based on financing through government-guaranteed suppliers' credits. This determination was prompted by the slow response of private investment, by the continuing uncertainties surrounding aid availability, by the critical agricultural situation, and by appreciation of the potential advantages of such an expansion program based largely on indigenous design and execution.[25] Such financing has been available in the past and was used in the Nangal project. It was taken up on a large scale, however, only with the Durgapur, Cochin, Barauni, and Namrup-II projects.

The primary benefit of this policy, given that suppliers' credits are available for a number of additional projects, from several sources of supply, is that the expansion program in fertiliser can proceed, even if government-to-government credits and direct private investments are not forthcoming, or are forthcoming only after considerable delay. Secondly, if variations in capital costs with changes in the bargaining position of the owner and the costs of delay in the conclusion of financial and contractual arrangements are taken into account, the real costs of capital under these suppliers' credits do not compare unfavourably. Thirdly, to a large extent the chicken-and-egg problem of finalising project design before knowing the source of finance is broken: equipment lists and specifications are to FCI's design, and it appears possible to get agreement that equipment not obtainable in the country providing the credits will be procured from a third country and supplied under the credit. This also has the effect of permitting standardisation to a greater degree, since the same plant design can be used even if the credit sources differ.

The foregoing description of the considerable strides made in one industry in project planning and management suggests a conceptual framework helpful in relating "infant industry economies" to the broader issue of absorptive capacity. The preceding pages have demonstrated potentially significant economies which can be realised as experience in investment planning in an industry accumulates and as many of the engineering, procurement, fabrication, and management functions are taken over indigenously. Over the transitional period, as additional functions are assumed bit by bit, the path of project costs is affected by (a) start-up costs involved in doing something for the first time, whether it be designing an ammonia synthesis unit or managing equipment procurement, and (b) costs stemming from loss of unity in management and control in the project and the consequent increase in problems of coordination and communication. Initial investments in an industry are likely to be implemented under unified "turnkey" contracts awarded to experienced foreign firms; as the process of import substitution in investment services approaches maturity, project control is likely to be re-unified under the owner or a domestic contractor. In the interim, the costs of disintegration in project management are likely to be felt in schedule delays due to failures in coordination as well as inexperience as new function are taken over.

There is little question but that the most important economies of the learning experience are those relating to schedule control and reduction of gestation periods, especially in inframarginal industries, and that the heaviest costs of the transitional period, as the Second and Third Plan experience has demonstrated, are those stemming from delays in the completion of projects. The calculations of the previous chapter illustrate this point vividly. It is extremely difficult to estimate the savings in capital costs that might follow from the process of import substitution and learning described above, but rough estimates solicited from a number of knowledgeable people connected with the industry suggest that 20 percent of project costs would be a reasonable figure, all things considered. In this context, "all things" include savings due to standardisation, lower engineering costs and service fees, lower procurement costs and construction overheads, and so on. It is interesting to note that this savings in capital costs, for inframarginal projects, would be completely offset by relatively small delays in project completion and attainment of full capacity. Valuing output at Rs 1000 per ton, a six months' delay in completion combined with a six months' delay in the attainment of an output rate of 90 percent of rated capacity would completely wipe out this capital savings. In actuality, of course, schedule slippages in many of India's new, heavy investment projects have been substantially greater than that. This suggests that one important aspect of time in the learning experience is simply in learning to manage time.

The preceding study also illustrates that the learning curve, in this area at least, cannot be regarded as a simple function of cumulated output, investment, or of time. Rather, the factors underlying transitional costs and the speed with which they are overcome depend on the decisions and efforts of key personnel. Recognition of this fact focusses attention on issues of industrial organisation and policy, and of a suitable market environment, to encourage and accelerate improvements in the ability to invest. In view of the high implicit rent on investment capabilities in many countries, this orientation is likely to be more fruitful than one which tacitly accepts limited absorptive capacity.

Finally, the preceding analysis has shed further light on the "make-or-buy" decisions which really characterise the problem of absorptive capacity. Viewing the development of domestic experience as a course which probably involves initial diseconomies and offers potential long-term savings, it is clear, first of all, that high rates of time discount operate in favour of the decision to import investment services in short supply, the more so the higher the initial diseconomies of the alternative course and the longer the expected learning period. Impediments to the pace or quality of investment cannot be easily tolerated in an economy short of capital, if potential foreign or domestic savings are thereby reduced or in industries which offer exceptionally high potential returns. The justification for substituting domestic skills depends critically on the ability of the economy to minimise cost and schedule overruns during the learning period and on the ul- timate savings that are expected to result. In turn, these savings are obviously related to the expected rate of growth in the industry, which will determine the pace of investment and the number of projects to which these savings will apply. In industries in which investments will be few and far between, it would make much less sense to promote the kind of indigenous development described above than in the rapidly expanding and potentially huge fertiliser industry. But, beyond these generalities, the essential point is that the strategy for particular industries in particular periods must be taken up individually.

The great advantage of importability is that it permits flexibility in planning, so that bottlenecks can be broken and domestic resources can be supplemented when they would otherwise be overstrained. In the Indian fertiliser industry, for example, a considerable use is being made of imported technical and engineering resources, especially in the private sector as local industrialists enter fertiliser production for the first time, while, simultaneously, considerable import substitution is taking place in the public sector. This may represent a quite rational response to the high value of time in the present circumstances of the Indian economy.

4 Time and the Choice of Techniques: A Study of Irrigation Programmes

This chapter is an attempt to illustrate the application of high rates of time discount to the choice between alternative means to the same end. Examples are drawn from the field of irrigation. The study first explores differences in the quality of irrigation service provided in several systems to emphasise that, when discount rates are high, the largest payoffs often flow from investments to extend or improve existing projects to obtain optimal utilisation. The study then presents comparisons among canal irrigation, private tubewell and state tubewell irrigation to show the significance of gestation periods in determining both capital intensity and profitability. The specific data used in this chapter were generated in a limited study of irrigation in the Punjab; the results and conclusions are intended to be only suggestive.

The conventional two-factor formulation of the choice-of-technique problem postulates alternative methods for producing a given time stream of output, some requiring more capital relative to labour than others. In practice, a great deal of care is required in the definition of output, which is always multidimensional. For a complex service like irrigation, this insistence on comparing equivalent values is particularly important, since the benefits a cultivator receives from an irrigation service depend on the *amount* of water provided, the *times* at which water is provided, the *reliability* and *certainty* with which this supply can be expected, and the degree of *control* by the cultivator over this supply. These are, as contemporary work implies, more appropriate inputs in an agricultural production function than simply "water."

In India, the characteristics and long-run value of the irrigation service have varied considerably among different methods of irrigation and even from location to location within the same project area. This chapter's study of irrigation conditions in sample areas in the Punjab, which compared locations irrigated from the major Bhakra-Nangal system, from state tubewells, and from small private tubewells in close geographical proximity, corroborated the existence and significance of these differences. The details of the study, including methodology and results, are presented in the appendices to this chapter. In all the canal-irrigated villages, deficiencies in the overall availability of water are perceived as a major problem. Water shortages, even under the extensive regime embodied in the Bhakra-Nangal project design, have long been recognised,[1] and have led to steps to tap supplementary sources. Even at authorised full supply levels, the water allowance at the distributory head throughout the system is no more than one cusec of capacity per hundred acres (one cusec = one cubic foot per second) to be irrigated in any one season. However, seepage losses have been estimated at 40 percent of the total flow between the distributory head and the cultivators' fields.[2] Moreover, the system has seldom been operated at full supply levels. Charts 1-3 indicate that the flow through the distributories in the sample areas has seldom averaged

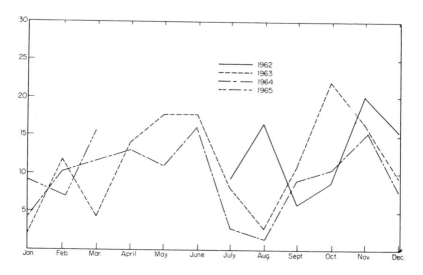

Chart 1   Khanna distributory: equivalent full supply days per month, 1962-1965.

more than two-thirds of capacity, even in peak seasons. Taking one cusec as equivalent to two acre feet of water per day, and assuming a standard watering of three acre-inches per acre, this implies that if the planned intensities of irrigation were realised, the minimum interval between waterings in a rotational system would be thirty-one days. This is probably not adequate to meet the peak water requirements of most irrigated crops; it is certainly not adequate to permit cultivators to follow their desired water use patterns.

Cultivators within canal-commanded areas have adjusted to this water shortage in several ways: by reducing the acreage irrigated out of total commanded holdings; by changing the cropping pattern or the frequency of water application; and by developing other, private irrigation sources. The first adjustment implies that the available water is distributed to

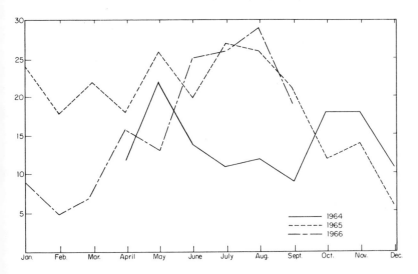

Chart 2   Ratta Khera distributory: equivalent full supply days per month, 1964-1966.

more cultivators with little intrinsic change in the total benefits provided, although there are undoubtedly economies of
scale in land preparation and agricultural operations related
to irrigation which increase the real unit costs of water to
the individual cultivator as the percentage irrigated of his
total holding declines. Moreover, the second form of adjustment is limited to some extent by the rotational system
which fixes the frequency of irrigation, even though the total
amount per acre can be adjusted by varying the number of
acres irrigated per turn.   Depth and frequency of irrigation
are substitutes to an extent limited by the carrying capacity
of the soil. In short, were the supply characteristics of canal
irrigation known with certainty, there would be considerable,
although not unlimited, possibilities for adjustment to it by
the users.

75

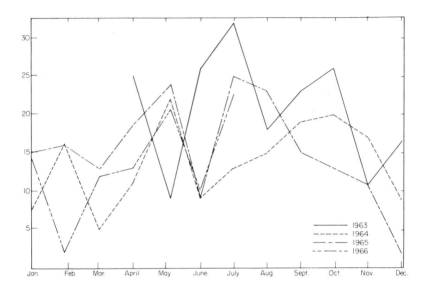

Chart 3   Kheri distributory: equivalent full supply days per month, 1963-1966.

This certainty has not been a conspicuous feature of the system in the past. Season to season, there has been considerable variability in the profile of water releases over time, and in most areas cultivators are not informed of the schedules early enough and definitely enough to make full adjustment. Schedules for releases are drawn up by the irrigation authorities area by area, taking into account crop requirements, actual rainfall, availability of water in storage and expected pattern of new influx, and requirements of power generation. Of course, derivation of an optimal schedule is an exceedingly difficult problem in dynamic programming under uncertainty,[3] and it is impossible to pass judgement on the optimality or nonoptimality of realised supply patterns. However, Charts 1-3 bear out the considerable degree of uncertainty facing the cultivators dependent on canal irrigation supplies. In all

76

TABLE 11. Hours Required to Irrigate One Acre[a]

Source of irrigation	Barwali Kalan L[b]	Barwali Kalan S[b]	Rahwan L	Rahwan S	Nasrali L	Nasrali S	Jallah L	Jallah S	Chimoon L	Chimoon S	Hijrawan Khurd L	Hijrawan Khurd S	Kirhan L	Kirhan S	Dayyar L	Dayyar S
Canal																
Near the outlet	3	4	2	1-1	½[c]	1-1			2	3	1½[d]	1-1	2			6
250 yards away	4	4½		1-1	¾[c]	1-1			2½	3½	2[d]	1-1	3			8
500 yards away	4½	5½		1-1	1[c]	1-1			2¾	4	2[d]	1-1	5[e]			10
Tubewell																
State																
Near the outlet							1½	2								
250 yards away							2	3								
500 yards away							3	3½								
Private	4½	5½	4		4		3½	4	4	6						
Persian wheel																
Single wheel	24	22	12		24		24									
Double wheel	12	n.a.	6		7		10									

[a] Of course, the time required to irrigate an acre depends on numerous factors, such as outlet size, slope of the channel, soil conditions, level of cultivator's field, and precise amount of water given. The above estimates were obtained in group conference and broadly average these factors, for a standard 2½ inch watering. Too much need not be made of the absolute magnitudes; the relatives and the ordering are the significant factors.

[b] "L" designates loamy soil; "S" designates sandy soil, as a broad distinction used in the interviews.

[c] There is no proper tail outlet at the end of the Khanna Distributary, and the unregulated flow is large.

[d] The clayey soils in this village cake and become quite slick in the channels.

[e] At a distance of 1000 yards from the outlet.

the three destributories, there is little concurrence in the annual supply profiles for the years examined, either in absolute or in relative magnitudes.[4] Fluctuations take the form both of temporary closures of minors by rotation and of diminished flow through open channels. The former results in missed water applications for the affected cultivators; the latter results in diminished availability for any application. Both are naturally disruptive of farm planning and crop maturation.

Even within the canal system, there are considerable differences in the characteristics of the service provided. Fundamentally, locations close to the proximate source of water have a twofold advantage over those at greater distance: they enjoy both a greater physical supply and a lesser degree of unreliability and risk. Thus, outlets near the head of a distributory tend to have an advantage over those near the tail, since weeding-up or other deterioration in the channel tends to increase water losses beyond the rates allowed for in project design. More significantly, fields located near any particular outlet tend to have advantage over those located at greater distance, because of considerable seepage losses in field channels, which may extend almost a mile's length from the outlet in some areas, and because the risks of other water losses and interruptions are greater at greater distances from the water source. Precise estimates of these losses in the sample area are unavailable, but the general estimates referred to above place seepage losses alone at from 30 to 40 percent of the water available at the distributory outlet, or from 20 to 25 percent of the total water let into the system at the source. Moreover, at the tail of the water course, losses are possible because of cuts or breeches in the channel upstream. Losses also occur if fields upstream are not irrigated in the rotation, since it takes time then to fill up the water course along the fallow or unirrigated tracts to reach the cultivators' holdings downstream. Similarly, it was reported that cultivators will often reserve some low-lying field to be irrigated last in their turn, in order to drain the channel as much as possible, thereby disadvantaging the next man in the rotation. For such reasons, proximity to the source reduces risk.

Some of the consequences can be seen from information collected from cultivators in the sample villages, and presented in Tables 11 and 12. It generally takes the cultivators whose fields are at greater distances from the outlet longer to give one acre a standard irrigation. Consequently, cultivators at greater distances typically irrigate a smaller fraction of their holdings in any season than do those nearer the outlet, both in dry and in normal years. The reported differences, moreover, were substantial; at approximately 500 yards from the outlet, the percentage of acreage irrigated in a commanded holding was typically only half that in holdings located at the outlets. This phenomenon is a reflection of the substantial differences in the irrigation service provided within a large project command area.

Much of what has been said about the characteristics of canal irrigation is applicable to irrigation by state tubewells, as they have been designed and operated in the Punjab. Overall water allowances have been about 2.85 cusecs per thousand acres of cultural command area, which is little higher than in the canal system. The distribution systems of these tubewells are naturally smaller in scale but have been designed on principles similar to the canals and are operated in much the same way; that is, the individual cultivator has had little control over either the amount or the timing of water flows,

TABLE 12. Percentage of Canal-Irrigated Acreage to Canal-Commanded Acreage, Normal Years and Dry Years[a]

Location	Barwali Kalan		Rahawan		Nasrali		Chimoon		Hijarawan Khurd		Kirhan		Dayar	
	N	D	N	D	N	D	N	D	N	D	N	D	N	D
Near the head	65	50	44	28	not sown		10	5	21	n.a.	20	13	50	33
150 yards away	28	21	37	20	42	22	8	4	21	n.a.	16	13	20	13
300 yards away	24	18	20	10	55	9	n.a.	n.a.	20	n.a.	n.a.	n.a.	n.a.	n.a.
500 yards away	13	7	17	6	40	10	n.a.	n.a.	n.a.	n.a.	14	5	8	6

[a] In the interview procedure, the normal year was specified as 1966-67, the dry year as 1965-66, to make the question more specific. The information was gathered from cultivators with holdings in the village and represents the percentages reported by them. The number of cultivators in each category is generally small, ranging from one to three. The data were verified by broad consensus in group meetings. The acreage irrigated with available water allotment depends on a number of factors, such as cropping pattern, soil moisture content, and weather conditions, but no attempt was made to control for these other variables.

nor have these flows been closely related to the requirements of optimal cropping patterns. Seepage losses and increasing risk have tended to result in appreciable advantages and disadvantages at different locations within the command area. Moreover, it appears that despite the greater potential of such groundwater pumping schemes for regular and assured patterns of water deliveries, there has still been a considerable amount of variability and uncertainty, caused primarily by power failures and load-shedding, and by frequent equipment breakdowns.[5] Consequently, cultivators regard state tubewell irrigation as essentially similar to canal irrigation.

This is not the case, however, with the small private tubewells and pump-sets which are being installed in large numbers where groundwater is available. These are under individual control, or, at most, jointly operated by a few farmers. This permits great flexibility in the intensity and the timing of irrigation supplies. Perhaps more significantly, it greatly reduces the uncertainty and risk surrounding water conditions and permits cultivators to plan with assurance for cropping patterns and agricultural practices involving higher inputs of water, fertiliser, and pesticides and to make permanent improvements on levelling, drainage, and water distibution. Typically, cultivators in the sample areas operate these installations to provide a more intensive irrigation service. It was ascertained that the acreage irrigated in any one season from a small set producing a flow of one-third to one-half cusec of capacity ranges from, say, ten up to twenty-five acres. This implies a minimum water allowance of one cusec per fifty to seventy-five acres. Also, seepage losses are less in the shorter water courses, and cultivators are free to operate their installations at full capacity levels during peak seasons. Cropping patterns under this more intensive irrigation regime tended to include more of such water-intensive crops as sugarcane, American cotton, and wheat, and less of millets, gram, and groundnuts.

The effect of such differences in *amount, timing, certainty,* and *control* of irrigation services on the long-run value of the product was investigated in the sample areas by developing estimates of the per-acre benefits under each kind of irrigation system and at different locations within the canal command. A detailed discussion of the method and the results appears in the appendix to this chapter. To recapitulate briefly, estimates were developed by cross-sectional comparisons of land sales and rental values within individual villages of lands unirrigated and irrigated by different means and at different locations. The theoretical justification for this procedure is straightforward; in a competitive market for land, rental value would approximate the expected annual economic surplus under optimal utilisation; sales value would approximate the capitalised value of expected future surpluses. Other things being equal, significant differences in the adequacy or reliability of water on particular fields would result in differences in their income potentials and hence in both sales and rental values. The practical justification for the procedure is equally straightforward: it is preferable to its alternative, which is to build up from detailed farm budgets *ex post facto* estimates of current surplus under best practice. This alternative has all the disadvantages of the present method—use of subjective estimates, observational errors, reliance on market data drawn from imperfect markets, and so on—and has several inherent additional disadvantages. Farm budget estimates are at best proxies for land value data, are subject to more serious sampling errors,

TABLE 13. Variation of Land Values with Irrigation Source in
Eight Punjab Villages in 1966
(Rs per acre)

	Four Ludhiana villages	Four Hissar villages
Average value, unirrigated land	3650	900
Average value, canal-irrigated land[a]	5900	2110
Average decline in value from head to tail of water course, canal-irrigated land	1100	470
Average value, tubewell-irrigated land	6800	—
Average value, state tubewell-irrigated land (1 village)	5000	—

[a]Evaluated at the approximate midpoint of the channel.

do not reflect cultivators' expectations about long-term locational advantages, and are more costly to collect. Other attempts
in India to use land value data in this way produced differentials
between irrigated and unirrigated land which broadly support
the findings of this study,[6] as do estimates derived from pooled
cross-sectional and time series regression studies of the impact
of irrigation on crop output.[7]

Table 13 presents summary data on the relation of land
value to water supply conditions, based on the detailed tables
in the appendix to this chapter. It is interesting that the
net benefits to the cultivator from irrigation in all forms

seems to be substantial. One reason for this is that the present demands for agricultural produce in India are large relative to the supply capabilities of unirrigated and previously irrigated land. Another reason is the strong technical and economic complementarity between irrigation and other modern agricultural inputs. Adequate and assured water not only raises the physical productivity of fertilisers and improved seeds (hence of pesticides and insecticides) but also lowers the cultivators' risks of supply failure under uncertain monsoon climactic conditions.

As a result, there is a strong correlation between the availability of irrigation and the use of fertiliser,[8] and, more generally, an expenditure per acre on all inputs that is higher on irrigated than on unirrigated acreage.[9] In the future, with the increased availability of high-yielding seeds and other complementary inputs, and no drastic fall in output prices, benefit levels should not be expected to decline greatly.

Per-acre benefits of irrigation from different sources also differ substantially, as do those at different locations within one system. Private tubewell irrigation is worth more to the cultivator than is canal water, except in fields very close to the canal outlets, despite the higher direct costs of tubewell irrigation. In canal areas, the fall in value from head to tail of water courses ranged from 19 percent to 22 percent of the average value of canal-irrigated land. These value differentials reflect and corroborate the differences in the irrigation service provided.

The major implication of this finding is that further investments to raise the productivity of existing projects may yield high returns. These value differentials, and the tremendous demand for private tubewell installations even within the effective command areas of canal and state tubewell systems, suggest that cultivators tend to prefer more intensive, more reliable, and more individually controllable irrigation services even at higher direct costs. Thus the possibility of adapting the operation of existing system to more optimal patterns at relatively modest incremental expense seems attractive for detailed exploration. Already there has been a huge capital investment in large irrigation projects: outlays on major and medium schemes have totalled about Rs 1200 crores in historic prices over the first three Plan periods, approximately 70 percent of total outlay on irrigation and 7 percent of all Plan expenditure. An irrigation "potential" of 18 million acres has been created, and an actual area irrigated of almost 14 million acres, the result of long periods of construction and a gradual process of adoption and adjustment by cultivators. The potential payoffs to be had from further steps to realise the utmost productivity from this capacity seem obvious. Thus, the Fourth Five year Plan Draft Outline states flatly: "The Fourth Plan will concentrate on consolidation of irrigation schemes already completed. A project should be considered completed only when all the actions necessary for securing optimum benefits have been taken."[10] Numerous studies have identified supplemental measures that can materially increase the benefits of existing systems: consolidation, or development of additional water sources where present supplies are inadequate; faster and more complete construction of distribution channels, including solution of land acquisition and minor engineering problems; consolidation of holdings in command areas; better land preparation, including levelling and provision for drainage; reduction of water losses through seepage in unlined distribution channels; better extension work to promote more efficient utilisation of available water; closer analysis and matching of water supplies and releases with the requirements of crops that cultivators will choose to grow in the command areas. These are all officially endorsed programmes to raise the productivity of investment in irrigation.[11]   Most would probably involve costs and gestation times that are small relative to the initial capital investment; indeed, some measures, such as providing more certainty to the cultivator about the profile of water releases, could be accomplished at almost negligible resource cost. Yet, these improvements would bring about considerable increases in the value of the service provided.

So much stress is placed on the conceptually obvious point that on a comparison of incremental costs and benefits there is a strong presumption in favour of improving and extending existing capacity rather than of creating more, because its applicability seems to be wider than the field of irrigation alone. Economists interested in development planning seem to have focussed primarily on investment in new plants and projects, although a major part of investment in any economy is on the renovation, modernization, extension, replacement, and balancing off of existing plant. With high rates of time discount, and particularly in sectors in which capital requirements are heavy and gestation periods long, this sort of relatively cheap and relatively quick-yielding investment should probably be given much more emphasis.

For the field of irrigation, the data generated in the sample villages of the Punjab have been used to explore one such measure to raise the productivity of existing projects: the lining of field channels to reduce water losses and cultivators' risks. This is obviously only one of a large number of improvements that might be attempted, but it is one which has been extensively discussed in the past. The results suggest that the incremental benefits would greatly exceed the incremental costs.

By field channel is meant the stretch in the distribution system from the outlet on the distributory or minor down to the place at which laterals and ditches take the water to individual fields. The latter are usually temporary constructions, since cultivators do not bring their water to the same fields in each season, and therefore lining would be uneconomical. The former, the distributories and minor, are sufficiently extensive that elimination of seepage from them would affect the local water table. Therefore, lining and pumping out groundwater by tubewells back into the canals are to an extent technical alternatives, and the relative costs seem to favor tubewells. This is not the case with field channels, since the water which does not seep from them is returned for the most part to the same local water table after seepage through farmers' fields, so that delivery of more water to the fields would not affect the local water table. Moreover, a major fraction of total seepage losses occurs in these field channels and small water courses.

The appropriate model to use in approaching this question would have two main elements; the first would be a mapping of the decrease in land values with distance from the outlet or source of water. Since channel lining would diminish the sources of this lower value, this mapping with opposite sign would form the base for valuing the potential gain. The second element would be an estimate of the geographical contour affected by the improvement. Total benefits would be estimated essentially by integrating the mapped value differentials over the contour of the affected area. The results would employ the capital costs of lining plus the discounted sum of maintenance and replacement outlays.

For Hissar District, Table 13 indicates that the average decline in value at a distance of twenty acre-lengths from the outlet along the main water course is Rs 470, i.e., about Rs 20 per additional acre removed. The detailed results in the Appendix indicate that there is an additional decline of about Rs 100 per acre for land located three or four acres off the main water course, reflecting the costs of conveying water over this path. These include not only further seepage losses but also problems of getting access along and on the fields owned by other cultivators, which can frequently be withheld. Therefore, it is appropriate to assume that the structure of land values with reference to their distance from the main water course would be unaffected. Also, it is not likely that lining would completely eliminate seepage or all the risks and disadvantages of the more distant location. Therefore, it has been assumed that lining would eliminate only one-half to two-thirds of the value differential, that is, Rs 12 to Rs 18 per acre.

Estimation of the geographical contour affected presents some problems. For one thing, the shape is relevant: to the extent that the acres irrigated are strung out in linear fashion from the outlet, the benefits (and costs) would obviously be greater, since there would be more channel per acre irrigated. In fact, it is clear from local irrigation maps that the linear pattern is more common, because of the design of the system to include large areas at low intensity of irrigation. Nevertheless, to be on the conservative side, a compact rectangular area has been assumed, which biases the benefit-cost ratio downwards.

Data were available for the distributories studied in Hissar on the capacity in cusecs, the culturable command area, and the average intensity of irrigation in 1963-64 and 1965-66 for each outlet along the distributory. These data indicate that the average gross area irrigated per cusec of capacity is at least 100 acres. Assuming an intensity of irrigation of 1.16 which is the average intensity on productive works in the Punjab in the past five years,[12] the net area irrigated might be about eighty-six. Therefore, a hypothetical outlet of one cusec capacity has been assumed, affecting alternatively a "gross" contour of 12.5 × 8 acres or a "net" contour of 11 × 8 acres. On this basis, calculation of the benefits is straightforward, and the tabulation below shows the capital value of savings, as estimated benefits of channel lining.

Per-acre savings	Total benefits	
	Gross acreage	Net acreage
Rs 18 per acre	Rs 11,250	Rs 8,712
Rs 12 per acre	Rs 7,500	Rs 5,808

On the cost side, at a high rate of time discount of about 15 percent, the more economical method of lining appears to be one which is less durable and requires more upkeep, but for which the initial capital expenditure is less. Lining with a bituminous mixture, assuming a channel of an average section of one square foot and replacement of the lining every eight years, would cost about Rs 232 for a distance the length of one acre square in shape.[13] These estimates lead to a range of benefit-cost relations, which are given below for lining of major field channels in canal-irrigated areas of the Hissar District in 1966.

Per-acre benefits	Benefit-cost ratios	
	On gross acreage	On net acreage
Rs 18 per acre	3.9 : 1	3.4 : 1
Rs 12 per acre	2.6 : 1	2.3 : 1

TABLE 14. Returns from Lining of Field Channels Expressed as the Discounted Present Value per Acre Affected, Hissar, 1966

Rupees per acre

Per-acre benefits[a]	On gross acreage	On net acreage
8 percent discount rate assumed		
(a) Rs 12	35	Rs 27
(b) Rs 18	73	Rs 60
15 percent discount rate assumed		
(a) Rs 12	56	Rs 37
(b) Rs 18	84	Rs 71

[a]This implies a benefit of Rs 12 or 18 for each *additional* acre distant from the water source.

If the applicable rate of time discount (assumed implicit in the capitalisation of benefits) is 8 percent, the use of more durable concrete slabs would be attractive. Discounted costs would be Rs 315 per acre length, and benefit-cost ratios would range from 2.8 : 1 to 1.7 : 1.

Table 14 presents the estimated returns in terms of the discounted present value of the activity per acre affected. These range from about Rs 27 per acre to Rs 84 per acre, which was over 9 percent of the average value of unirrigated land in those villages in 1966.

Although the soils in this district are sandy and the water courses long, the absolute benefits are relatively low because agriculture is unproductive in the region. In Ludhiana, where the marginal productivity of water is greater, the return would be higher. Of course, if canal systems were designed more compactly for a higher intensity of irrigation, the costs of such improvements would be substantially less.

The conventional formulation of the choice-of-techniques problem also postulates identical time-streams of output from alternative means. This can be rationalised as the result of an implicit process of discounting and normalisation, but it obscures important considerations. Differences in the durability of the productive facilities, differences in the time required for project completion or in the time needed to increase output to full capacity levels, can often be the determining factors in the choice among alternative means. Especially for investment activities which, like irrigation in India, offer large potential returns, the speed with which benefits can be obtained is often the most important single determinant of success. Naturally, the higher the rate of time discount, the more attractive will be the quick-yielding method.

In irrigation, for example, it can be shown that one of the major economic disadvantages of systems which serve large numbers of cultivators has been the slow pace of development of irrigation potential. This problem has been extensively investigated by the Government of India, so that it is possible to identify with some confidence the elements involved.[14] The problems of project management discussed in the previous chapter are present in an acute form, especially if the project is considered to include not only the physical completion of structures but also the completion of institutional changes to acquire or consolidate land, to provide the needed credit facilities, and to promulgate information about the proper adjustment to new water conditions among the cultivators; the completion of steps to make available complementary inputs like fertilisers and seeds; and the completion by cultivators of individual investments in land improvements and small water courses to permit utilisation of irrigation supplies.

Various agencies are involved in the implementation of this broadly defined project, and the synchronisation of its different phases has proven extremely difficult to achieve. Major group-water systems include the backward and financially weak cultivators along with the more progressive, so the pace of adoption is naturally slower. Moreover, conflicts of interest over the location of outlets, the alignment of field channels, the construction of water courses, etc., must be resolved before full use can be made of irrigation potential, and this also slows the pace of development. By contrast, individual tubewells and pump-sets are installed only when the cultivator is sufficiently motivated to invest a substantial sum, and thereafter he has a strong financial interest in maximising the return on this commitment. For this reason, there is little or no development problem.

Further, with water as with other agricultural inputs, there is considerable evidence to suggest that the pace at which cultivators will adopt is strongly related to the expected return, with a substantial minimum return necessary to overcome uncertainty and risk. Thorough adjustment to irrigation implies not only a change in cropping pattern and cultural practice but also considerable outlay and effort on land preparation. Therefore, although it may possibly have been true, as irrigation authorities have maintained in the past, that under Indian conditions the maximum return *per unit of water* has been obtainable by spreading it thinly over a large area, the relatively small incremental benefits *per acre* that have resulted may not be sufficient inducement to prompt large numbers of individual cultivators to take rapid steps to use the irrigation potential provided. Thus, there tends to be a correlation between the potential per-acre benefit and the rate of growth of acreage irrigated. Both tend to favor small, individually controlled schemes.

In order to explore the practical significance of these differences in development time, in the spirit of Chapter 2, rough estimates were developed for the total benefits for three means of irrigation in the Punjab sample area. Although the results are couched in the language of benefit-cost analysis, it is important to emphasise that the purpose is sensitivity analysis and *not* an appraisal of the economic worth of the Bhakra-Nangal system nor of the state tubewell program. The Bhakra system is vast, a multi-purpose development with important joint costs and products, which has brought a qualitative change in economic life to large areas. Similarly, thousands of state tubewells have been installed over large tracts, with important consequences not only for irrigation but also for the management of the underground water table. It would be rash to attempt overall *ex post facto* judgments of the results, particularly on the basis of such scanty and superficial information as that presented here. All that is intended is to shed some light on the structure of the benefits and costs, in terms of the time-streams involved.

For reasons already discussed, it appears that despite the higher unit costs of irrigation by small individual tubewells and pump-sets, they are, where groundwater is readily available, the most profitable form of irrigation. On the benefit side, as indicated in Table 13 for Ludhiana District, the incremental land value for private tubewell-irrigated land is Rs 3150 per acre, in contrast to Rs 2250 per acre for canal-irrigated land in the same villages, despite the higher direct private costs of such water.[15]

On the cost side, investment requirements will vary according to boring depth and conditions, engine and pump specifications, differences in structural features, and installation charges. Broadly, the total costs for tubewells in the Ludhiana area with a bore depth of 120 to 200 feet, a water table

TABLE 15. Estimated Benefits and Costs of Private Tubewells in Ludhiana District in 1966

	Rupees
Capital costs, with perpetual replacement	
using 8% discount factor	5700
using 15% discount factor	4500
Per-acre net benefits, excluding capital costs	3150
Benefit-cost ratios	
Assuming 10-acre command area	
assuming 15% discount factor	7.0 : 1
assuming 8% discount factor	5.5 : 1
Assuming 20-acre command area	
assuming 15% discount factor	14.0 : 1
assuming 8% discount factor	11.0 : 1
Discounted present value of the project per acre irrigated	
Assuming 10-acre command area	
assuming 15% discount factor	2700
assuming 8% discount factor	2580
Assuming 20-acre command area	
assuming 15% discount factor	2825
assuming 8% discount factor	2865

depth of 20 to 30 feet, three-inch discharge capacity, and five hp electric motor will be in the range of Rs 2500 to 4000, as of 1966. Diesel-powered sets might cost Rs 1000 more.[16] Using the higher cost figure with an allowance for perpetual replacement, the total cost ranges from Rs 4500 to Rs 5700. Table 15 presents benefit-cost calculations for effective command areas of ten and twenty acres.

It is apparent that the ratio of net benefits to capital costs is very high, ranging from 5.5 : 1 to 14 : 1, depending on the number of acres assumed to be irrigated, on the average, by such a small tubewell. The discounted present value of the stream of net returns appears to be in excess of Rs 2500, or more than 50 percent of the total investment costs. These results might seem questionable, on the grounds that returns of this magnitude would prompt an overwhelming demand for tubewells in these areas or a rapid bidding up of land prices in anticipation of subsequent installation, or both. However, there has indeed been a rapid adoption of tube- well irrigation. Investment has been limited by supply con- straints rather than by any weakness in demand. In the case that an electricity distribution line need be installed, the procedures for estimation of the costs and approval of the prospective customer's application generally have taken one or two years to complete; if a loan is required, it will be forthcoming through official channels only after delays of up to one year. Also, drilling equipment, pumps, and engines have been in short supply. On the other hand, cultivators have been willing to install wells on holdings of as little as three acres, and, in Hissar District, have been willing to pay Rs 15,000 for a well to irrigate thirty acres. Moreover, the data presented in the Appendix indicate that unirrigated land in Ludhiana, where groundwater is assured, is in fact capitalised at much higher rates than already irrigated land. Therefore, the results are not at variance with market behaviour.

This high profitability does not imply, of course, that development of other forms of irrigation should be ignored. Groundwater resources are large in some areas and absent in others, and data concerning the extent of this resource are incomplete. Also, in many areas the water table is considerably affected by the operation of the canal irrigation system, making the two alternatives interdependent. More fundamentally, it has already been argued that steps to improve the productivity of existing irrigation systems and major projects, on an incremental cost-benefit comparison, would also show high profitability. The results do suggest, however, that steps to remove impediments to private tubewell development would be greatly rewarded. Moreover, the apparently high rates of return raise questions about the *proper* degree of caution about groundwater development in areas where (*a*) major and medium perennial irrigation development is contemplated in the future, (*b*) data on the water table are lacking, and (*c*) holdings may be too small to support installations of optimal scale.[17] The higher the potential payoff and the rate of time discount, the less important become such risks that might reduce the benefits of such investments in the future, and the more important it becomes to secure the immediate returns.

In contrast to private tubewell irrigation, the structure of benefits from state tubewells illustrates the effects of slower development. According to Planning Commission studies, this slower development is attributable to a number of factors, including delays in energising wells and in completing water courses, problems of land acquisition, unreliable water supplies, inadequate credit facilities and extension facilities for cultivators, and other obstacles equally associated with canal irrigation.[18] Unfortunately, information in the sample was available only for two wells in one village. In terms of performance, however, one of these has been quite similar to the hundred-odd state tubewells installed in Eastern Ludhiana in the same period (1955-1956), while the other has been quite clearly superior. The summary data in the tabulation below on the average hours operated and acreages irrigated annually for Jallah and all state tubewells during the period 1955-1956 to 1963-1964 bear this out.[19]

	Summer		Winter	
	Acreage	Hours	Acreage	Hours
Wells in Jallah Village				
Number 9	263	1480	320	1398
Number 10	83	530	110	735
101 wells, Eastern Ludhiana				
Samrala area	91	586	140	777

Thus, well number 10 has been about 10 percent below average in terms of performance, while well number 9 has been about twice the average.

Per-acre benefits have been calculated on three alternative assumptions: one, that the per-acre benefits are equal to three-fourths those under private tubewells; two, that they are equal to those under canal irrigation; three, that they are equal to the absolute magnitudes found in Jallah Village. Future benefits are estimated as the differential land sales value between unirrigated and state tubewell irrigated land. It might be thought that these estimates would underestimate future irrigation benefits, since adjustment to new water supply conditions at present, more favourable relative prices and better availability of fertilisers and improved seeds is still in progress. However, there is persuasive evidence that in the valuation of land, cultivators effectively discount the probability of future gains in productivity and earning capacity. In the Ludhiana villages, as the basic data in the appendix to this chapter indicate, the rental income from irrigated land is capitalised at the ratio of about 28 : 1, while that from unirrigated, but irrigable, land is capitalised at a rate of about 40 : 1. This difference is what one might expect, since in an area where the water table is accessible, the potential *future* gains in earning power will be greater on unirrigated than on already irrigated land. More fundamentally, a capitalisation ratio of 28 : 1 with a constant and perpetual income stream implies a discount rate of only 3.7 percent; a ratio of 40 : 1 implies a rate of 2.6 percent. It is difficult to accept, even granting noneconomic demands for land ownership, that cultivators who borrow and lend at rates ranging from 8 percent to well over 20 percent per year discount income from land so moderately. On the other hand, if one assumes that cultivators apply a discount rate of 10 percent to future earnings from land, it would follow that they expect something like a 7 percent annual growth of income from non-irrigated and 6 percent from irrigated land. This seems more reasonable. Therefore, it has been assumed in this study that future increases in productivity are adequately reflected in land values.

For past years it could not be assumed that per-acre benefits remained approximately constant in real terms. The figures in Table 16 show that the hours of operation per acre irrigated have risen markedly, by a factor of more than three, over the decade of their operation. In the early years, before the command areas of state tubewells were reduced, they operated scarcely three hours per acre irrigated. This could have sufficed for at most one standard watering in the course of the season for each acre irrigated. In contrast, the present levels are adequate for three to four waterings. To compensate for this marked shift in intensity, the acreages irrigated

TABLE 16. Annual Acreages Irrigated and Hours of Operation: State Tubewells in Jallah and Samrala-Doraha

Year	Jallah no. 9				Jallah no. 10			
	Summer		Winter		Summer		Winter	
	Acreage	Hours	Acreage	Hours	Acreage	Hours	Acreage	Hours
1955-56	37	119	116	217	18	55	21	75
1956-57	53	362	119	505	19	78	17	56
1957-58	92	303	211	670	21	127	260	250
1958-59	613	1815	556	1405	147	409	105	244
1959-60	595	1826	506	2201	171	886	216	523
1960-61	313	2507	370	2868	83	606	92	771
1961-62	253	2260	396	2958	110	781	103	748
1962-63	250	2454	326	2453	110	920	84	570
1963-64	165	1667	283	2703	64	900	93	1127
1964-65	243ᵃ	2508	313ᵃ	2986	102ᵃ	1467	95ᵃ	1155
1965-66	200ᵃ	2058	356ᵃ	3402	126ᵃ	1772	116ᵃ	1398

Average: 101 wells, Ludhiana

Year	Summer		Winter	
	Acreage	Hours	Acreage	Hours
1955-56	15	48	20	48
1956-57	33	124	33	118
1957-58	34	111	124	322
1958-59	98	415	163	413
1959-60	128	616	229	842
1960-61	137	1015	201	1277
1961-62	120	756	170	1074
1962-63	127	927	152	1106
1963-64	89	966	170	1792

Indices of hours of operation per acre irrigated

Year	Jallah no. 9		Jallah no. 10	
	Summer	Winter	Summer	Winter
1955-56	31	20	22	30
1956-57	66	44	29	27
1957-58	32	34	43	8
1958-59	29	26	20	19
1959-60	30	45	37	20
1960-61	78	81	52	69
1961-62	86	78	50	60
1962-63	95	79	60	57
1963-64	100	100	100	100
1964-65	100ᵃ	100ᵃ	100ᵃ	100ᵃ
1965-66	100ᵃ	100ᵃ	100ᵃ	100ᵃ

ᵃAssumed on the basis of hours of operation.

TABLE 17. Calculated Benefits, Jallah State Tubewells, Nos. 9, 10

	Gross acreage/net acreage (Rs lakhs)	
	at 15 percent	at 8 percent
Estimated past direct benefits, accumulated on "adjusted" basis		
Tubewell no. 9		
At Rs 110/acre (canal)	8.4/7.2	6.0/5.2
At Rs 103.5/acre (private tubewell)	7.9/6.8	5.7/4.9
At Rs 90/acre (Jallah, actual)	6.9/5.9	4.9/4.2
Tubewell no. 10		
At Rs 110/acre (canal)	2.2/1.9	1.6/1.4
At Rs 103.5/acre (private tubewell)	2.1/1.8	1.5/1.3
At Rs 90/acre (Jallah, actual)	1.8/1.6	1.3/1.1
Estimated future benefits, based on land value differentials		
Tubewell no. 9 (G.A.=550)		
At Rs 2250/acre (canals)	12.4/10.6	12.4/10.6
At Rs 2362/acre (private tubewell)	13.0/11.2	13.0/11.2
At Rs 1400/acre (Jallah, actual)	7.7/6.6	7.7/6.6
Tubewell no. 10 (G.A.=250)		
At Rs 2250/acre	5.6/4.8	5.6/4.8
At Rs 2362/acre	5.9/5.1	5.9/5.1
At Rs 1400/acre	3.5/3.0	3.5/3.0
Estimated total benefits		
Tubewell no. 9		
Canal basis	20.8/17.8	18.4/15.8
Private tubewell basis	20.9/18.0	18.7/16.1
Actual Jallah basis	14.6/12.5	12.6/10.8
Tubewell no. 10		
Canal basis	7.8/6.7	7.1/6.2
Private tubewell basis	8.0/6.9	7.4/6.4
Actual Jallah basis	5.3/4.6	4.8/4.1

were deflated by an index of the hours of operation per acre, then per-acre benefit levels based on differential land rental values were applied. Calculations were carried out on both gross acreage and net acreage bases, using the same figure of 1.16 for the intensity of irrigated cropping. On these assumptions, Table 17 shows the estimated past, future, and total benefits from these state tubewells.

The more rapid and fuller utilisation of the superior well has evidently resulted in past benefits, over the first decade of operation, almost four times as high as those obtained from the more average well. Should the disparity in utilisation rates continue, future benefits will be about twice as high as on the better well. These results show the effect of high rates of time discount in emphasising early differences in performance: those in the first years are weighted much more heavily in the calculation of total benefits. Put another way, despite the assumption of perpetual replacement, absolute differences in benefits stemming from the first decade's performance account for half of the total differences in benefits.

To translate this comparison into cost-benefit vocabulary, the net revenues and losses on working expenditures have, first of all, been neglected. In fact, state tubewells with few exceptions have been unable consistently to earn financial returns adequate to cover their working expenses. The sums involved, however, are less than Rs 2000 per year, negligible even in the aggregate. Capital costs of these tubewells have been expressed in 1966 prices and accumulate to 1966 at alternative rates of interest, then adjusted by the discounted cost of perpetual replacement,[20] every twenty years starting in 1976. These costs amount to Rs 3.8 lakhs per well, using an 8 percent discount rate, or to Rs 6.2 lakhs per well, using a 15 percent discount rate.

Table 18 indicates that one of the tubewells studied in this village, the one slightly inferior in performance to the average well in the district, is of marginal economic value. The other, which has been utilised considerably more intensively and

TABLE 18. Benefit-Cost Calculations for State Tubewells in Jallah

| | At 15 percent discount | | At 8 percent discount | |
	On gross acreage	On net acreage	On gross acreage	On net acreage
Discounted present values in Rs per acre				
Tubewell no. 9				
Low estimate	1510	1350	1600	1490
High estimate	2600	2440	2650	2540
Tubewell no. 10				
Low estimate	-360	-760	280	155
High estimate	720	320	1420	1195
Benefit-cost ratios				
Tubewell no. 9				
Low estimate	2.4:1	2.0:1	3.3:1	2.7:1
High estimate	5.2:1	4.5:1	8.1:1	7.0:1
Tubewell no. 10				
Low estimate	0.9:1	0.7:1	1.3:1	1.1:1
High estimate	2.0:1	1.8:1	3.2:1	2.8:1

which waters twice as large an area, is apparently quite inframarginal in investment value. This suggests that those wells which can be fully and rapidly utilised are economically sound. One might infer that additional outlays to accelerate utilisation of the typical well would be generally profitable. One is also tempted to infer that solutions like those attempted in West Pakistan, where large tubewells pump water into canal distribution systems to supplement surface water supplies might be profitable, since full utilisation of wells could fairly easily be obtained. (This ignores possible beneficial effects on the water table from such programmes.) As the wells have been operated in the past, the generally lower range of cost-benefit ratios for state tubewells as compared to private installations reflects primarily the faster and fuller realisation of returns from the latter.

The same distinction on benefits can be applied to canal irrigation from the Bhakra system, but further distinctions on cost are also required. As the figures in the last two columns of Table 19 indicate, the pace of completion of the various phases of the vast storage and distribution system, as well as the pace of adoption by the cultivators, have been gradual. Since cultivators typically irrigate only part of their commanded holdings, and perhaps different fields in different years, it might be thought that the impact of irrigation on land values would be wider in area than the net area irrigated in any particular year. Therefore, figures on gross acreage as well as net acreage have been presented, using the ratio of 1.16 : 1 as a conversion factor. It is interesting that the rate of growth of utilisation in the enormous Bhakra system has not been obviously slower than that in the comparatively miniscule state tubewells. This underscores the point that the rate is closely related not to scale as such but to the synchronisation of project phases and the attractiveness of the service offered to the cultivators in the command area.

Average per-acre benefits were assumed to be the same, in real terms, in past years as in 1966, an assumption which probably overstates past benefits. Estimates of per-acre annual current benefits were based on the differences in *land rental* values between canal-irrigated and unirrigated land. Since data on rental values were available only for the Ludhiana villages, the capitalisation ratios prevailing in Ludhiana were used with land sales value data in Hissar to develop estimates of cash rental values there. The differentials betweeen canal-irrigated and unirrigated land come to Rs 110 per acre in Ludhiana and Rs 50-60 per acre in Hissar, reflecting the generally higher levels of agricultural productivity in the former area. These differentials were taken as extreme values

103

TABLE 19. Expenditure on Irrigation and Acreage Irrigated in Bhakra System

Year	Capital outlay on irrigation accounting, Rs crores[a]	Capital outlay 1965-66 prices, Rs crores	Net current revenues, Rs crores	Net current revenues 1965-66 prices, Rs crores	Total gross acreage irrigated, 000 acres	Net area irrigated, 000 acres
1948-49	7.40[b]	17.91[c]	—	—	—	—
1949-50	4.08	7.70	—	—	—	—
1950-51	4.51	8.35	-0.01	-0.02	—	—
1951-52	4.69	8.23	-0.01	-0.01	—	—
1952-53	11.56	18.65	+0.03	+0.05	—	—
1953-54	22.09	36.82	0.00	0.00	—	—
1954-55	19.11	30.33	-0.17	-0.27	9.78	8.43
1955-56	11.40	17.81	-0.41	-9.64	11.48	9.90
1956-57	7.89	10.11	-0.21	-0.26	13.50	11.64
1957-58	9.85	12.63	-0.42	-0.54	16.65	14.35
1958-59	9.90	12.07	-0.34	-0.41	19.52	16.83
1959-60	5.55	6.77	+0.59	+0.72	21.15	18.23
1960-61	7.52	9.06	+0.06	-0.07	18.71	16.13
1961-62	4.75	5.40	+0.45	+0.45	22.43	19.34
1962-63	1.94	2.16	+0.46[d]	+0.45	22.57	19.46
1963-64	1.18	1.27	+0.47[d]	+0.45	25.00[e]	21.55
1964-65	0.38	0.40	+0.49[d]	+0.45	25.00[e]	21.55
1965-66	0.38	0.38	+0.51[d]	+0.45	25.00[e]	21.55

[a]Figures supplied by Bhakra-Beas Control Board.
[b]Cumulative to the end of 1948/49.
[c]Calculated by backwards extrapolation, application of cost index, and recumulation over time.
[d]Assumed in such a way as to make figures constant at 1960-61 levels in real terms.
[e]Assumed.

in a range with which to estimate per-acre benefits for the entire Bhakra system.

Taking the higher figures as a basis for calculation, the rewards to any acceleration of the pace of utilisation can be made clear. If, for example, there had been a one-year acceleration, in the sense that the starting date of irrigation would have been unchanged but the amount of acreage irrigated every year shifted backwards in time by one year, then total accumulated past benefits would have been higher by Rs 110 crores at 15 percent interest and by Rs 50 crores at 8 percent interest. Table 19 indicates that these sums amount to approximately 15 to 20 percent of the total benefits realised to date. Again, these estimates merely serve to emphasise the high potential returns to steps and investments which will promote this more rapid utilisation.

Total benefit figures in Table 20 were derived by assuming that in the future total gross acreage irrigated by the system will remain constant at twenty-five lakh acres. This is a reasonable assumption, since any major increases in acreage will depend on the development of additional water supplies, and these supplementary investments can be evaluated separately. Future benefits were valued by applying the differentials in land *sales* value, as in the case of tubewells, using the figures for Ludhiana and Hissar as extremes in a range.

Comparison of the structure of costs in the Bhakra canal system and in state tubewells also will illuminate the role of time in the choice among alternative techniques. The conventional formulation of the problem postulates different factor proportions among alternative efficient methods, different ratios of "capital" to labour. The cost of capital should obviously be construed as the cost of resources tied up: the "waiting" or "round-aboutness" in the productive process. Thus, labour expended in advance of production contributes to the capital cost just as does expenditure on

TABLE 20. Estimated Total Benefits and Costs of Bhakra-Nangal System Canal Irrigation, in Current Prices

	Rupees crores[a]	
	at 15 percent	at 8 percent
Accumulated capital costs	1106	503
Net direct benefits		
Accumulated past benefits		
at Rs 60 per acre		
on net area irrigated	234	178
on gross area irrigated	272	206
at Rs 110 per acre		
on net area irrigated	430	323
on gross area irrigated	499	375
Discounted future benefits		
at Rs 1210 per acre (Hissar)		
on net area	261	261
on gross area	303	303
at Rs 2250 per acre (Ludhiana)		
on net area	485	485
on gross area	563	563
Estimated total benefits		
low estimate		
on net area	495	439
on gross area	575	509
high estimate		
on net area	915	808
on gross area	1062	939
Total benefits per acre		
low estimate		
on net area	1980	1720
on gross area	2300	2020
high estimate		
on net area	3660	3240
on gross area	4250	3760
Total costs per acre	4424	2012

[2]One crore = 10 million.

equipment. Gestation periods are of the essence of the choice of techniques problem.

Between the major storage and canal project and the state tubewell, for example, the former's long construction period is the major reason for its higher capital intensity. On the reasonable assumption that after ten years the development time for these tubewells and for the Bhakra system as presently constituted is more or less complete, one can obtain a fair measure of the relative costs by comparing the present value of the capital outlay per acre irrigated in the two systems, that is, the accumulated annual capital outlays expressed in current prices. (It should be recalled that irrigation began on one within a year of the start of irrigation from the other.) The basic data for the Bhakra system are presented in columns one and two of Table 19.[21] The difference between current revenues and expenses is negligible and has been neglected, as for state tubewells. The present value of annual capital outlay per acre irrigated, for canal and state tubewells, in current prices, at 8 and 15 percent discount, is shown below (in Rs per acre):

Irrigation source	At 15 percent	At 8 percent
Bhakra system	4424	2012
Tubewell no. 9	1127	691
Tubewell no. 10	2480	1520

In this calculation, the higher cost estimates for tubewells have been used and perpetual replacement has been assumed. It is obvious that the capital costs of canal water are higher in real terms. This is because capital must be, or was, tied up for longer periods in the construction of such a massive system. In fact, if one considers the *undiscounted* capital costs of the two alternatives, as in the tabulation below, canal irrigation then appears the less capital-using. The undiscounted capital costs per acre for irrigated canal and state tubewells in current prices were as follows:

Irrigation source	Rupees per acre
Bhakra system	720
Tubewell no. 10	806[a]-874[a]

[a]No discount factor has been applied to initial investment, but replacement expenditures have been discounted at 8 and 15 percent. Otherwise, of course, the total costs with perpetual replacement would be infinite.

The obvious conclusion is that the best way to reduce the capital intensity of such projects is to complete them more rapidly. For this reason, the Planning Commission has stated very strongly that for the Fourth Plan the first priority in irrigation shall be to complete projects already in progress.[22] It remains only to add that short-term drops in the availability of funds do not weaken this case and justify stretch-outs in project work enforced by budgetary cuts. On the contrary, by raising the implicit rate of interest, such tightenings of the savings constraint strengthen the relative advantage of projects which can be brought to fruition with comparatively little additional investment and with comparatively little additional lag. Therefore, steps to accelerate project completion should have even higher priority.

This conclusion also exposes the fallacy underlying attempts to conserve capital by adopting extremely labour-intensive means of construction in large public works projects. Capital is saved, of course, only if the more labour-intensive alternative can be completed with no substantial increase in the overall construction time. This is usually not the case. Therefore, even if a very low real social cost is attached to the use of unskilled labour, the probability of any significant conservation of capital is small. Suppose that in the construction of Bhakra system, for example, more use had been made of unskilled labour. The greatest relative use of such labour in a gigantic irrigation project in India was probably in Nagajunasagar in Andhra Pradesh, an earth and masonry construction in which it was used extensively for materials handling and construction. There, the fraction of unskilled labour costs in the total was about 33 percent; in other major projects, the fraction was between 10 and 20 percent.[23] Thus, even if one assigned a zero social cost to the use of unskilled labour, the potential savings in capital costs could probably not exceed, say, 20 to 25 percent of the total. If such extremely labour-intensive designs and construction methods should add just one year to the completion time, which would not be the least unlikely in the light of Indian experience, these savings would be almost completely wiped out: at a 15 percent discount rate, a 20 percent savings in capital costs would be Rs 200 crores, while, using the low estimate of benefit-cost ratio of 1 : 1, the loss in benefits would be Rs 159 crores. If completion were delayed by two years, an overall loss would result. Also, if unskilled labour should be positively priced or the benefit-cost ratio were higher, this kind of step would be less attractive. This point does not always seem to have been firmly grasped by project designers and economists in India.

To recapitulate the general results of this chapter is simple, since the main conclusion is only this: high rates of time discount favour projects that can be completed and brought to full production quickly. Its application, as the

examples given for one sector in this chapter have attempted
to show, probably offers substantial payoffs, to actions
which will raise the value of output on existing capacity
and accelerate the completion and utilisation of new investments.

Appendix to Chapter 4

Methodology of the Study of Benefits

The use of cross-sectional observations on land values to estimate irrigation benefit has been used by other researchers and needs no further
theoretical explanation.[1] In this study, however, reliable observations
could not be obtained from transactions data, so that interview methods
were required. Rental values are usually unrecorded. Recorded sales
values tend to be both scanty and unreliable. In any particular village, the
number of land sales during a year will almost invariably be too few to
support a cross-sectional analysis, while the pooling of observations from
different years is inadvisable, since both the agricultural structure and
the general price level have changed substantially. Recorded sales values
may be exaggerated or understated, according to circumstances. The pre-
emption clause in the Punjab land laws often leads to overstatement if
the purchaser feels his purchase may be challenged. The recorded price
on intrafamilial transactions may be inaccurate. Duties on land transactions lead to understatement. Under these circumstances, primary reliance was placed on group interviews involving leading cultivators in the

1. For example, L. M. Hartman and R. L. Anderson, "Estimating the Value of
Irrigation Water from Farm Sales Data in North-eastern Colorado," *Journal of Farm
Economics,* 44 (February 1962) 207-212; E. Renshaw, "Cross-Sectional Pricing in
the Market for Irrigated Land," *Agricultural Economic Research,* 10, no. 1 (January
1958), 14-19; and V. Ruttan, "The Impact of Irrigation on Farm Output in California,"
Hilgardia, 31 (July 1961), 69-111.

villages and others, to arrive at consensus estimates on rental and sales values. This procedure had not only the virtue of necessity; it also took advantage of three concrete factors: one, in any village, there are more bids, contemplated acquisitions, and related market testing than actual transactions; two, every financially strong cultivator tends to be a potential buyer, and therefore acts as an informal appraiser—of his own lands and those of potential sellers and renters in the village; three, the level of knowledge in the village, or, at least, within homogeneous village groups— about matters of strong common interest is high. The study attempted to use this village knowledge.

The detailed methodology can best be explained by recounting the interview procedure. In each village, interviewers[2] first obtained from the village *patwari* or from Tehsil headquarters a map showing the orientation of canal distributories and minors, the location of outlets, watercourses, state tubewells, and other geographic features. These were verified in the field and supplemented if necessary. Then, the assistance of the *gram sevak*, the Block Development Officer, or other extension official was enlisted to convene a gathering of from ten to twenty of the more knowledgeable cultivators in the village. In this group, interviewers first obtained further information on the location of private tubewells and persian wells, the general regions within the village with reference to broad soil conditions, flooding or alkalinity, proximity to roads and habitations, location of electricity connections, and other relevant geographic features. The group was then asked to supply information on the operation and problems of irrigation systems, which were invariably met with considerable interest and concern. Only after establishing some degree of rapport was an attempt made to explore the pattern of land values in the village.

In exploring the variations in rental values in village lands, the operative concept was the going cash rental for the use of the land and water rights. For canal-irrigated land, this would include all the water turns authorised for the acreage taken. For privately irrigated land, this would include a proportionate share of the available water. It was stipulated that the

---

2. Field interviews were carried out in the autumn of 1966 by Mr. Tilak Raj and Mr. Gurdev Singh Sidhu, M.Sc., graduates in farm management from the Punjab Agricultural University in Ludhiana. Both interviewers are native to the Punjab, with experience in extension work.

taker would be assumed to pay the direct water costs in addition to the rent. For canal or state tubewell-irrigated land, this would mean the water rates; for tubewell-irrigated land, this would be the cost of diesel fuel or an appropriate share of the electricity bill.

In exploring the variations in sales value, the operative concept was a more subjective one: the greatest amount the cultivators, by consensus, would be willing to pay for the particular acreage. Since respondents tended to be among the more knowledgeable and progressive cultivators in the villages, the upper limits of their offers would tend to approximate the capital values of income potential under best practice. Also, since the land market in the Punjab is today a seller's market, reliable bid figures are easier to obtain. Most sellers part with their land only under the pressure of circumstances. Many cultivators, when asked their selling price, reply that they have no intention of selling; if pressed, the reply that if forced to sell, they would take what they could get. As before, ownership of land was stipulated to include the burden of all land taxes and assessments, and all water rights including a proportionate share in water from private wells at direct cost.

In the group interview, estimates were obtained for both rental and sales values for land under alternative irrigation sources present in the village and for unirrigated land. For lands irrigated by canal or state tubewell, estimates were obtained for acreage near and at various distances from outlets and watercourses. Interviewers attempted to arrive at a true consensus by first eliminating divergent interpretations of the question. As a general rule it was specified that land be considered of average fertility for the prevalent soil type in that part of the village, that it not be adjacent to existing holdings of the buyer, that it have no specific defects, that it have adequate access to village habitations and roads, and so on. By this process, it was possible to narrow down the range of estimates at first advanced in the large group to a consensus on the representative variations in value with reference to the source and location of irrigation water.

In the next step, interviewers went on foot, with from two to four cultivators with holdings in a particular area within the village, and obtained further estimates of land values at various locations along watercourses and field channels. This provided both a check on the previous, more general observations, and a feeling for the magnitude of influences other than water. Results were recorded in terms of average sales and rental values and a range of values encompassing the impact of other factors. The average figures are not true statistical means of observations, but rather representative figures based on the consensus estimates generated by the interviews.

At this stage, it is appropriate to review the advantages and disadvantages of this methodology and this choice of estimators. The alternative, which has been tried in many studies in India,[3] is to build up from farm accounts a measure of the difference in net income from irrigated and unirrigated land in a sample year or years. This involves, first, estimating the effect of differences in cropping patterns and yields and valuing this at some prevailing price set. It also involves estimating the difference in purchased and nonpurchased inputs, including seed, fertiliser, water, fuel, draft and mechanical power, hired and family labour, imputed interest on capital, and so on. These inputs are valued at some market or imputed prices. The difference of this different set of values is taken to be the annual net income due to irrigation.

First, this approach calls for a large amount of data, while the land value approach calls for only one bit, for every holding in the sample. Second, this approach rests on the realised results in the sample year or years, raising acutely the problem of fluctuations in weather and market conditions. The land value approach rests on expectations, which are almost certainly more stable, and which in themselves embody a valuation of risk elements. Third, this approach escapes none of the valuation problems involved in deriving estimates from imperfect markets. If local markets for land are imperfect, so are markets for family farm labour, management, fodder, bullock power, farmyard manure, and the outputs of certain crops, all of which are marketed

3. A number of studies were sponsored by the Research Programmes Commission of the Planning Commission: K. S. Sonchalam, *Benefit-Cost Evaluation of the Cauvery-Mettur Project* (Delhi, 1960); S. K. Basu and S. B. Mukherjee, *Evaluation of Damodar Canals, 1959-60* (Calcutta, 1963); B. Singh and S. Misra, *New Benefit-Cost Analysis of the Sarda Canal System* (Bombay, 1965); Malhotra and Sanjeeva, *Evaluation of Benefits of Irrigation, Gang Canal* (Delhi, 1960); B. Singh, *The Economics of Minor Irrigation,* Lucknow, to be published.

only to a limited extent.[4] Fourth, the use of an indirect estimate which is essentially a proxy for the economic rental value of the land, built up by the addition of a number of variables subject to errors of measurement, is probably subject to greater sampling variability than direct observation on the rental value itself.

The use of land value data is subject to the major disadvantage that it is impossible to obtain reliable observations unless there is some reasonable market for land. In parts of India, therefore, the technique would probably not be usable. Assessment by the villagers themselves also has its disadvantages, the most serious of which is the suspicion and reticence that are frequently encountered by outsiders enquiring about vital village affairs like land and asset holdings. Even the use of local interviewers and elaborate efforts to establish rapport probably did not completely overcome this problem. Another salient problem is that of identifying and eliminating the numerous extraneous factors influencing land values. In some villages, lands near the habitations are considered more fertile because they receive more than their share of the village nightsoil; in others, they are considered less valuable since they are more subject to damage by wandering cattle. In other villages, lands far from the habitations are less valued since women returning from them are in greater danger of assault and must therefore leave their work earlier. Some relatively low-lying lands are more prized since they are easier to irrigate; others are less prized since they tend to flood. It is obvious that in a formal cross-sectional study designed to isolate the effect of favourable water supplies a large sample and a large number of variables would be required. The interview technique simulated this process of control over extraneous variables by identifying them in the course of discussions, assessing the sensitivity of land values to them, and then either simply assuming them away or assuming a specific state for them.

4. In fact, some of the studies sponsored by the Research Programmes Committee include a rental charge as a cost factor in calculating the net benefits of irrigation. See Government of India, Planning Commission, Research Programmes Committee, *Criteria for Appraising the Feasibility of Irrigation Projects* (New Delhi, 1964). To subtract this differential rent should lead to observations centered on zero, and the use of this procedure goes too far to explain why in some of the studies negative net income differentials between irrigated and unirrigated land were recorded occasionally.

Sampling Procedure, Information on Sample Villages, and Detailed Results

The unit of observation in this study was the village, and the sample consists of eight villages. Four lie in Ludhiana District in central Punjab, and four lie in Hissar District in what is now the state of Haryana. All fall within the command area, and are watered by, the Bhakra-Nangal system, although some in Hissar also obtain water from other, older canals. Bhakra-commanded villages were intentionally selected in order to obtain information about lands watered by irrigation systems of fairly recent origin. These villages first obtained Bhakra water in 1954-55 and perennial supplies in 1961-62.

Ludhiana and Hissar districts present strong contrasts in agricultural conditions and structure.[5] Ludhiana receives more rainfall, has a larger percentage of land under irrigation, has plentiful supplies of groundwater in a high water table, and has as a consequence more well irrigation. Hissar has been, until the completion of the Bhakra-Nangal, largely a dry tract, with little and unreliable rainfall and little usable groundwater. Relatively more acreage is devoted to dry crops like bajra (millets), gram (chick-peas); in Ludhiana, more acreage is planted to major food crops like maize, wheat, and paddy. In Ludhiana, holdings tend to be smaller and output per acre larger. The consumption of fertiliser per acre is larger. Ludhiana is also one of the Intensive Agricultural Development Programme (IADP) Districts, implying, presumably, a more intensive extension effort. In Hissar, on the other hand, the process of agricultural change has been more rapid, with relatively widespread shifts in cropping patterns following the availability of irrigation.[6] These two districts were initially selected primarily to encompass areas within the Bhakra command with and without adequate supplies of groundwater, and which represented strong contrasts in agricultural conditions approximating the extremes to be found within the Bhakra command.

Within each of the districts, subdivisions were chosen. In Ludhiana, the Samrala-Gobindgarh tract in the eastern section was selected, since that is

5. See National Council for Applied Economic Research, *Cropping Patterns in the Punjab* (Delhi, 1966).
6. Ibid., p. 65

by-and-large the only area within the district in the Bhakra command (falling under the First Main Line Circle). Here, there is much less flooding and waterlogging than in the North and West, where canal irrigation is of much longer standing. In Hissar, the Ratia and Fatehabad subdivisions, lying north to south in the central part of the district, were selected. These fall under the Second Main Line Circle and include sandy tracts near the Rajasthan border.

Within each subdivision, data were obtained from irrigation records and the advice of irrigation and extension officials was solicited to select distributories the operation of which, in terms of intensity of water use and cropping patterns, was representative of those in the subdivision as a whole. The distributory selected in Ludhiana was the Khanna Distributory; that in Ratia, the Ratta Khera Distributory; that in Fatehabad, the Kheri Distributory. The Khanna Distributory is quite similar to the others in the same area, with respect to both intensity of irrigation and cropping patterns on irrigated land. Intensity of irrigation on the Ratta Khera and the Kheri, on the other hand, seems comparatively low. This was not fully realised at the time of selection, since the data from irrigation records were being compiled and primary reliance was placed on information provided by irrigation authorities. On investigation, the explanation was found, for the Kheri, in a large tract of very sandy soil near the tail which is not effectively irrigable with available supplies. No villages were selected from this area. For the Ratta Khera, the problem was found to be an area in the middle reaches of the commanded area which is regularly flooded by a nearby drainage canal, and is not irrigated. Again, since no village was selected from this area, the problem was not serious.

Along each distributory, villages were selected from near the head and near the effective tail reaches, to capture possible variations in water supply conditions with distance from the source. All the distributories chosen were about twenty-five miles in length. Preference was given to villages in which alternative sources of irrigation, such as tubewells, were present. It was also specified that the villages lie directly on the distributory, so that outlets would be in the village. These conditions narrowed the choice in each area to at most three or four villages, from which the choice was essentially random. In addition, one village was selected in Ludhiana off the canal system, in which two state tubewells are in operation, and one village in the middle reaches of the Khanna Distributory.

TABLE 21. Background Data on Sample Villages

Village and district	Population, 1961	Total area, acres	Gross cropped area, 1965	Date of consolidation	Date of electrification	Distance from town, miles	Distance from Pucca Rd.	Start of Bhakra irrigation	Distance from head of distributory, miles	Distance from tail of distributory, miles
Ludhiana										
Barwali										
Kalan	1140	974	1335	1952-53	1962	9	2	1954	6	22
Rahawan	1264	2153	2747	1950-51	1952	1	0	1954	18	10
Nasrali	1523	1833	1900	1950-51	1965	8	1½	1954	28	0
Jallah	1060	1060	1539	1953-54	1962	15	½	—	—	—
Hissar										
Chimmon	319	982	450	1959-60	—	18	0	1956	0	25
Hijrawan										
Khurd	3088	11,230	10,142	1962-63	—	9	4	1956	25	0
Kirhan	2991	5647	6131	—	—	4	4	1954	4	29
Dayyar	1235	4874	2520	1962-63	—	11	3	1954	26	7

TABLE 21. (Continued)

Village and District	Total canal outlet capacity cusecs	Total canal culturable command area	Designed irrigation intensity, percent	No. of tubewells installed, electric/diesel 1955-59	60-63	1964+	Average outlet diameter, inches	Average HP motor	Average of depth bore, feet	Water table depth, feet	No. of Persian wheels
Ludhiana											
Barwali Kalan				0/6	2/9	2/8	3	5	130	32	23
Rahawan				52/0	10/0	10/2	3	5	125	30	5
Nasrali				0/0	0/4	3/2	3	5	110	15	80
Jallah				0/0	6/3	10/2	3-4	5-7½	80-100	9-15	8
Hissar											
Chimmon	1.13[a]	471[a]	62	0/0	0/0	0/17	4		80-100	30	0
Hijrawan Khurd	9.60	3495	62	0/0	0/0	0/3	6	45	150	80	0
Kirhan	10.50[ab]	5083[a]	62	—	—	—	—	—	—	—	—
Dayyar	10.50[ab]	5007[a]	62	—	—	—	—	—	—	—	—

[a]The figures include the total capacity outlet discharge and the total command area of all outlets serving the village either in part or exclusively, on the distributory under study. That is, area within the village commanded from other distributories is excluded, while area outside the village commanded by the same outlets that command the village are included.

[b]There are seven outlets serving the village. It is assumed that the average outlet capacity is 1.5 cusecs.

The sample villages are listed below. Table 21 presents general background information about them. Those in Ludhiana are smaller, more densely populated, and have been consolidated a decade earlier. All have recently obtained electricity connections, which are enjoyed by none of the villages in Hissar. The Ludhiana villages fall in Zone I of the Bhakra command, the restricted perennial zone. A water allowance of 2.25 cusecs of discharge capacity at the distributory head per 1000 acres of cultural command area was allowed for this zone, with the system to operate on the average at 43 percent capacity in the summer and 69 percent in the winter. This was based on an assumed intensity of irrigation of 45 percent and implies a duty of water of 200 gross irrigated acres per cusec of discharge capacity at the head. Hissar falls within Zone III, the unrestricted perennial area, for which water allowance was 2.75 cusecs of capacity at the head per 1000 acres of cultural command area, with average operation at 80 and 72 percent of capacity in the summer and winter respectively.

It will be seen that the Ludhiana villages are substantially dependent on well and tubewell irrigation. Rahawan, which received electricity in 1952, has the largest number of tubewells; Nasrali, which was electrified in 1965, has the smallest. Typically, the pumpsets are relatively small, with the capacity to deliver a flow of up to one-half cusec. Most of the powered wells are of recent origin; most of the persian wheels had been installed a decade or more ago, and no more are being constructed. In Hissar, only Chimmon and Hijrawan Khurd, which benefit from the higher water table near the Ghaggar River, have wells for irrigation. They are all very recent and very popular, though larger, deeper, and more expensive to install. A list of the sample villages follows:

Name and area	Sources of Irrigation
Hissar District	
Ratta Khera Distributory	
Chimmon	Canal, private tubewell
Hijrawan Khurd	Canal, private tubewell
Kheri Distributory	
Kirhan	Canal
Dayyar	Canal

Name and area	Sources of Irrigation
Ludhiana District	
Khanna Distributory	
Barwali Kalan	Canal, well, private tubewell
Rahawan	Canal, well, private tubewell
Nasrali	Canal, well, private tubewell
Other	
Jallah	State tubewell, well, private tubewell

Some of the villages had noteworthy particular characteristics. In Ludhiana, Barwali Kalan and Nasrali lie on the fringe of the "Groundnut Belt" that extends from west to east across the tehsil in predominantly sandy soil. In this belt, groundnuts are the major crop on unirrigated kharif acreage. Nasrali, which is actually, although not in design, the last village irrigated from the Khanna Distributory, has also an alkalinity problem in some parts of the village. Affected holdings are naturally much less valuable. *Rahawan*, in which groundnuts are not an important crop due to the prevalence of irrigation and the quality of the soil, nonetheless lies next to the major groundnut market, Khanna Town. In fact, Khanna Model Town encroaches on a corner of village land, and this proximity has unquestionably lifted land values. Also, Rahawan boasts a typically prosperous and progressive farmer, probably an ex-officer of the military or civil service, well connected with the powers that be. This is reported to be one reason why Rahawan obtained electricity well in advance of surrounding villages.

In *Chimmon*, there is a flooding problem in one part of the village, now separated from Bhakra-irrigated areas by a bund, caused by overflow from the Rangoi drainage canal. At the tail of the same distributory, *Hijrawan Khurd* is a very large village containing five distinct hamlets. The inhabitants are mostly families displaced from Pakistan at partition; holdings are, therefore, tending to be large—up to and over 100 acres— and the farmers tend to be progressive.

121

TABLE 22. Land Values under Different Situations, Ludhiana District, Khanna Distributory of Bhakra Canal (Rupees per acre)

	Barwali Kalan				Rahawan			
	Land Values		Rental values		Land values		Rental values	
	Average	Range	Average	Range	Average	Range	Average	Range
Canal-irrigated area								
Distance from the outlet along main course								
Within 2 acres	5500	4500-6000	180	175-200	7500	7000-8000	250	280-350
350 yards away	5200	4000-5500	150	150-175	7500	7000-8000	250	200-250
600 yards away	4200	4000-4500	110	100-125	6800	5500-7000	210	180-240
Distance from the main water course along lateral water channels								
Near head								
1-2 acres away	5200	5000-6000	180	170-180	—	—	—	—
3-4 acres away	5200	5000-6000	160	160-180	—	—	—	—
5-6 acres away	4800	4500-5000	150	125-160	—	—	—	—
Near tail								
1-2 acres away	4000	3800-4200	100	100-120	—	—	—	—
3-4 acres away	3800	3800-4000	100	100-120	—	—	—	—
5-6 acres away	3600	3500-3800	85	85-100	—	—	—	—
State tubewell-commanded area								
Within 2 acres	—	—	—	—	—	—	—	—
350 yards away	—	—	—	—	—	—	—	—
600 yards away	—	—	—	—	—	—	—	—
Private tubewell								
Not within reach of canal water	5500	5000-6500	210	200-225	8200	8000-8400	300	250-300
Private Persian wheel								
Not within reach of canal water	5000	4500-5500	180	180-200	7800	7500-8000	250	210-250
Unirrigated land	3000	2500-3200	60	50-70	4500	4200-5000	100	80-130

TABLE 22. (Continued)

	Jallah				Nasrali			
	Land values		Rental values		Land values		Rental values	
	Average	Range	Average	Range	Average	Range	Average	Range
Canal-irrigated land								
Distance from outlet along main water course								
Within 2 acres	—	—	—	—	5800	5500-6500	280	275-350
350 yards away	—	—	—	—	5000	4800-5500	250	240-300
600 yards away	—	—	—	—	4500	4000-5000	230	200-280
Distance from main water course along lateral water channels					If alkali soils			
Near head								
1-2 acres away	—	—	—	—	2000	2000-2500	100	90-100
3-4 acres away	—	—	—	—	1500	1200-2000	90	80-120
5-6 acres away	—	—	—	—	1000	900-1100	80	70-100
Near tail								
1-2 acres away	—	—	—	—	—	—	—	—
3-4 acres away	—	—	—	—	—	—	—	—
5-6 acres away	—	—	—	—	—	—	—	—
State tubewell-commanded area								
Within 2 acres	5500	5500-6000	250	250-350	—	—	—	—
350 yards away	5000	500-5500	200	200-250	—	—	—	—
600 yards away	4800	4000-5000	175	120-200	—	—	—	—
Private tubewell								
Not within reach of canal water	5500	5000-6000	285	200-300	8000	7000-8500	250	200-250
Unirrigated land	3600	2500-4100	110	100-120	3500	2500-4000	150	100-200

123

TABLE 23. Land Values under Different Situations, Hissar District, Ratta Khera Distributory of Bhakra Canal (Rupees per acre)

	Chimmon (Village at head of distributory) Land values of					Hijrawan khurd (Village at tail of distributory) Land values of				
	Paddy land	Dabar weed land	Cotton land	Wheat land	Bajra gram land	Paddy land	Dabar land	Cotton land	Wheat land	Bajra gram land
Canal-irrigated land										
Distance from outlet along main water channels										
Within 2 acres of outlet	3000	1700	3200	2500	2200	2500	1500	3800	2300	1800
Within 10 acres of outlet	2800	1500	3000	2300	1900	2200	1200	3500	2000	1500
Within 20 acres of outlet	2400	1200	2700	2100	1700	2000	1000	3000	1900	1350
Distance from main water course along lateral field channels										
Near head										
1-2 acres away	3000	1700	3100	2500	2200	2500	1500	3800	2300	1800
3-4 acres away	2950	1650	3000	2400	2100	2450	1400	3700	2000	1700
Near tail										
1-2 acres away	2400	1200	2700	2100	1700	2000	1000	3000	1900	1300
3-4 acres away	2350	1100	2650	2000	1600	1900	900	2900	1800	1250
Range of land values										
Near outlet										
Adjacent	3000	1700	3200	2400	2200	2500	1500	3800	2400	1800
Not adjacent	2700	1400	2700	2200	1900	2400	1200	2600	2200	1700
Near tail										
Adjacent	2400	1200	2600	2100	1700	2000	1000	2500	1850	1300
Not adjacent	2200	800	2000	1900	1600	1800	800	2200	1650	1150
Unirrigated land (level)										
Adjacent areas	1600	550	1700	1600	1000	1500	500	2000	1600	900
Not adjacent area	1450	450	1500	1400	900	1400	400	1900	1450	800
Sand dunes	–	–	–	–	800	–	–	–	–	600

TABLE 24. Land Values under Different Situations, Hissar District, Kheri Distirbutory of Bhakra Canal (Rupees per acre)

	Kirhan (Village at head of distributory) Land values of				Dayyar (Village at tail of distributory) Land values of			
	Cotton land	Paddy land	Wheat land	Gram land	Cotton land	Paddy land	Wheat land	Gram land
Canal-irrigated land								
Distance from outlet along main water course								
Within 2 acres of outlet	2500	2800	2400	2000	2100	2500	2000	1500
10 acres away	2200	2600	2200	1500	2000	2300	1900	1350
20 acres away	2000	2000	2000	1200	1800	2100	1700	1200
Distance from main water course along lateral field channels								
Near head of main water course								
1-2 acres away	2500	2800	2300	1900	2100	2400	2000	1500
3-4 acres away	2400	2600	2200	1400	2050	2350	1950	1450
Near tail of main water course								
1-2 acres away	2000	1900	2000	1200	1800	2100	1700	1200
3-4 acres away	1800	1600	1900	1150	1750	2000	1600	1000
Range of land values								
Near the outlets								
Adjacent	2600	2800	2400	2000	2200	2550	2050	1200
Not adjacent	2200	2650	2250	1950	2000	2350	1850	1000
Near the tail								
Adjacent	2100	2050	2100	1300	1850	2100	1700	1200
Not adjacent	1800	1700	1850	1150	1650	2000	1650	1150
Unirrigated land								
Adjacent areas	1000	800	900	600	700	900	850	600
Not adjacent areas	850	700	800	550	600	800	750	500
Sand dunes	–	–	–	450	–	–	–	400

Table 22 presents the data on land values by source of irrigation and location for the four villages studied in Ludhiana; Tables 23 and 24 the data for the villages in Hissar. Between the two, the format differs in two important respects. In Ludhiana, it was possible to collect estimates of cash rental values, since this is a fairly common form of lease. In Hissar, it is more common to sharecrop or to pawn land against cash loans, and information on cash rentals was impossible to obtain. Also, the estimates for Hissar villages are broken down into "paddy land," "cotton land," "gram land" and so on. This format was adopted during the course of interviews, because farmers there were more insistent on the importance of such variations in soil characteristics. The categories reflect not hard and fast use categories but rather local descriptions of variations in soil type. By contrast, in the estimates for Ludhiana, this sort of variation is incorporated into a general estimate of the range of land values. Also, since field channels are longer in Hissar, longer intervals from the outlet were adopted in the questioning.

5 Accelerating Development Programmes: A Study of the Madras Vasectomy Programme

Previous chapters have attempted to show that, in the context of high rates of time discount, speedy realisation of benefits from investment projects is a crucial factor in determining the actual pace of economic growth, and also to show how this should colour the interpretation of comparative advantage, balanced growth, infant industry economies, absorptive capacity, and choice of techniques in India. This chapter deals with a critical nonindustrial programme—family planning—to show how these high rates of time discount affect the framework for decision-making and implementation in programmes with large potential payoffs, heavy administrative requirements, and large measures of uncertainty.

Much has been written by experts in public administration in, for, and about the government of India on problems leading to delays in the process of administrative decision-making and programme implementation. In each Plan, such delays affecting important programmes have been identified as a critical challenge for the period ahead. A great deal of attention has been given to review of outmoded work methods and financial and administrative procedures, to personnel policies, staffing patterns, the organisation of decision hierarchies, and other matters internal to the administrative structure.

This study in the field of family planning emphasises two important aspects of the *environment* of administration in India, as opposed to the internal administrative structure, which greatly influence administrative performance. One is that the Government of India is embarked on a drive for rapid development in a country of vast dimensions and diversity, of widespread poverty and backwardness among the masses, and of only twenty years' experience as a sovereign nation. As a consequence, many of the programmes the nation is undertaking are unique. Certainly, this is true in the field of family planning. Not only was India the first nation to adopt a comprehensive population control programme as a matter of official policy but, more importantly, this programme is an attempt to reverse demographic trends dramatically by halving the birth rate within a single generation in a population overwhelmingly rural, isolated, and illiterate. When this attempt was begun, little was known about the relevant demographic parameters, the sociological nexus of fertility, attitudes towards family size and contraception, or the avenues of mass motivation in the Indian population. The technology of contraception was, by and large, developed in and suitable for a more affluent and sophisticated society. Such a programme lay well beyond the scope of traditional functions of government in India, and an administrative machinery for large-scale implementation was totally absent. As a result, during the first two Plan periods, efforts were confined very largely to research, experimentation, collection of data, and the conduct of pilot projects. This was a natural reaction to the uncertainty which clouded all facets of the programme.

The impact of uncertainty on the decision process is largely a negative one. This is especially so in the field of population control, which lies close to the centre of social norms and family structure and which yields benefits and risks that are difficult to measure and compare. Despite the high priority placed on the programme, the effect of uncertainty has been to delay decisions and to shift them towards conservatism, towards cost-minimising or risk-minimising solutions, or towards research activities as opposed to action programmes. This tendency is reinforced by shortages of current, reliable, and relevant data useful for programme evaluation and the lack of an appropriate explicit framework for decision within which benefits, risks, and costs both financial and social can be estimated, weighed, and compared. In the absence of such a framework, the danger is that even such data as may be available will not be brought to bear on a decision problem and that different agencies concerned will implicity attach quite different weights to the various factors involved.

The second aspect of the environment of administration which this study emphasises is the rapid expansion of functions imposed on government by the goals of development and the voracious demands of development programmes for personnel trained and skilled in fields hitherto quite foreign to the administrative structure. The Extended Family Planning Programme adopted in the Third Plan, for example, calls for a veritable army of doctors, nurses, social workers, and health educators to work in close proximity to the people throughout the country;[1] in addition, experts in communications, publicity, and the use of mass media are required to support the programme, plus an apparatus for the production and distribution of contraceptive supplies and a greatly expanded machinery to provide statistical services, and financial and general administration. This, for one programme alone, implies a gigantic burden of recruitment, training, and deployment and has constituted a principal impediment to progress under the scheme. Most states have experienced difficulties in finding enough doctors and paramedical personnel willing to work under difficult and professionally unstimulating conditions in rural areas and enough competent social workers and educators at approved salary levels to carry out the extremely difficult tasks involved. As a result, coverage up to the end of the Third Plan remained spotty.[2] In a pessimistic view of the situation, one team of observers made the following assessment: "Because of the sheer size of the operation, the difficulties in providing training, accommodation, transport and other facilities and the reluctance of doctors and other professional personnel to serve in rural areas, it seems unrealistic to expect that the plan can be implemented generally within the next decade, even if it were given strong and effective support from the central and State governments."[3] This serious view of the problem is shared by most of the state family planning authorities, who point to shortages of key personnel as one of their most pressing difficulties.

Because of the importance of early results, this tends to place a premium on measures which contribute to programme goals without requiring additional administrative machinery, more specifically, measures which use more intensively existing machinery and those which bring into play other institutions within government and in the private community. To an extent, such measures have been adopted. In some states, extensive use has been made of voluntary organisations. In some, private doctors and clinics have contributed greatly to the programme. Some industrial establishments and similar institutions have actively promoted family planning among their employees. Conventional contraceptives like the condom are produced and marketed through private channels. By and large, however, primary reliance has been and continues to be on the construction of a governmental administrative structure to carry out virtually all aspects of the job. This is an orientation which must have a cost—and sometimes a very considerable cost—in time lost while building an apparatus with which to produce results.

At the present time, the principal constraint on the family planning programme is *lack of effective demand.* It is not lack of support either from government or from the general population: family planning has had a high priority in all Plans, and surveys among all sorts of people have indicated favourable attitudes towards limitation of family size and family planning as such. However, there is a wide gap between knowledge and approval on the one hand and regular practice on the other. The principal constraint is not financial, although certain states have professed difficulty in finding their minor share of the financial resources for the programme. In every Plan period to date, expenditures have fallen far short of budgetary provisions; and, for the Fourth Period Plan, the government of India has pledged all the money that can usefully be spent.[4] It is not a shortage of clinical facilities and medical personnel, although large areas and large segments of the population are without convenient access to sterilisation, the intrauterine device (IUD), or even conventional contraceptives and family planning counsel; existing facilities for sterilisation and IUD insertion are now operating at levels greatly below full capacity, although their target populations have scarcely been touched. For example, at the end of the year 1965-66, there were 2516 units for sterilisation in India and 2353 units for IUD insertion. During that year, 542,000 sterilisations were performed and 804,000 loops were inserted. This implies a rate of 18 sterilisations per clinic per month, and 28 IUD insertions: *about one a day or less.*[5] By contrast, an experienced surgeon with a little support can easily perform twenty vasectomies in a day. Similarly, a practitioner can easily insert fifty loops in a day, including thorough examination beforehand and adequate explanation or reassurance afterwards. Therefore, presently available clinical facilities are grossly underutilised; doctors supposedly engaged full time on family planning work often quite reasonably spend most of their time on other medical activities; and were the clients forthcoming from the untapped target populations within reach of these facilities, they could easily be accommodated.

Developments at the end of the Third Plan period have served only to emphasise this point. The loop programme, which had such a promising beginning, has faltered in almost all of the states where initial response was encouraging: Gujerat, Punjab, West Bengal, and Kerala are notable examples. This has been attributed to adverse publicity from dissatisfied users unprepared for uncomfortable side effects, from midwives and local practitioners whose support had not been ensured, and to difficulties in reaching into lower income stratas and rural areas to convince women to come forward, once the most highly motivated potential acceptors had all been accommodated.[6] It has been recognised that a key element is the availability of personnel able to work effectively with lower-class (and often lower-caste) women in the villages, to win their confidence and overcome the doubts that have been planted about the programme, in order to translate general interest in family planning into effective demand for the loop or another contraceptive device.

This discussion provides a background for the study of a specific family planning programme—the use of commissioned, door-to-door field workers to promote vasectomies in Madras State—the results of which are presented below. First, the employment of these canvassers, as they are called, strikes at the critical problem of generating more effective demand to utilise fully available clinical facilities and to reach a scattered, illiterate, and disadvantaged target population. Second, this programme complements the working of the regular administrative structure by enlisting the private initiative of a self-recruited group of workers drawn from the same socioeconomic strata as those of the target population and operating outside, but under the control of, the bureaucratic machinery. Third, this programme generated a certain amount of controversy which juxtaposed its proven effectiveness in increasing the number of vasectomy cases and a number of social costs which allegedly resulted from the use of commissioned promoters outside the administration. It therefore represents an interesting decision problem and provides an opportunity to examine the consequences of uncertainty and the lack of a framework for decision appropriate to the complexities inherent in family planning programmes.

As constituted in 1966, the essence of the canvasser programme was the payment of Rs 10 to the canvasser for every man he brought to a surgical clinic who was accepted for vasectomy. Six or seven canvassers were attached to each of the four full-time clinics operating in Madras City and more to each of the twelve Districts in the State. Canvassers were appointed by the district medical officers, or by the superintendents of the city hospitals where clinics are located. The only formal qualifications were that canvassers should themselves have undergone vasectomy. Beyond this, the medical officer had to convince himself that the candidate was familiar with the nature of the operation, the hygienic prescriptions the patient should follow, and government policy regarding the eligibility of patients to undergo vasectomy and that the candidate was of good character and appearance. Recruitment was through newspaper advertisement or word of mouth. Tenure was on good behaviour; violation of policy by the canvasser could result in suspension or loss of licence. The payments to canvassers were part of a general incentive system in the vasectomy programme, by which the patient received Rs 30 after the operation in compensation for loss of wages, the Panchayat Union in the rural areas received Rs 20 if cases were sponsored by it, and the individual Panchayat received Rs 10 to cover the cost of transportation, tea and tiffin, and other incidental expenditures for cases sponsored by it.

In urban areas, canvassers were drawn from the ranks of labourers and petty clerical or commercial occupations, in rural areas from tenant farmers and agricultural labourers.[7] Their educational attainment rarely exceeded the primary level, and their identification—in dress, manner, and association—tended to be not with the lower civil service but with the common man. Most were attracted to the job by the expectation of increased earnings, and these expectations were usually fulfilled. There was relatively little turnover among canvassers; most of those working in Madras City in 1966 had been doing so for at least five years; most of those working in the districts in 1966 were hired in 1964-65, during the first year in which the canvasser programme was extended to provincial areas.

The incentive payment of Rs 10 ($1.33) was sufficient to evoke a considerable organisational development among canvassers.

Those attached to city hospitals typically had a number, ranging from five or six to over one hundred, of agents working more or less closely with the canvasser to locate prospective patients and see them through the operation. These agents were rewarded with a fraction, typically half, of the Rs 10 fee, out of which they may have spent a certain amount on transportation and refreshment for themselves and their patient on the way to the hospital. Many of these agents operated in Madras City; most, however, operated either in the villages where they live or in a range of villages in the vicinity. Thus a canvasser maintained contacts and assistants over a wide geographic area. It was not uncommon for a Madras canvasser to draw cases from a 100-mile radius: some regularly visited the neighboring states of Andhra Pradesh and Mysore. The agents' functions differed considerably from canvasser to canvasser; some merely passed on the information about men desiring vasectomies or men having large families and small incomes; some provided the canvasser with valuable local contacts and introductions when he visited the village; others functioned virtually as independent entrepreneurs, bringing in patients themselves to Madras for "delivery" to any licensed canvasser willing to split the fee. Sometimes these agents were recruited by the canvasser from relatives, caste brothers, or acquaintances. Most typically, however, they were men who had previously been brought in for vasectomy by the canvasser, and were then invited to help recruit more patients in return for a monetary reward. In essence, the system in rural areas and provincial towns was the same, except that canvassers tended to operate on a somewhat smaller scale in a more limited area.

The mode of operation of the canvasser was, in the first place, an arduous one. Most worked a six- or seven-day week, using the weekends for excursions into the villages, travelling extensively by train or bus and spending several nights a week away from home. Having located a prospect, either through agents or the good offices of a village leader, the canvasser would spend several hours attempting to win his confidence and to overcome the apprehensions of the man or his wife. If they could not finally be convinced, the canvasser would return one or more times within a few months to try again. If a prospect agreed, then the canvasser or an agent would arrange to accompany him to the hospital—immediately, if possible—sometimes paying for overnight lodgings if necessary, and would shepherd the man through the interviews and the operation at the clinic. Some of the largest operators arranged group meetings in the villages, at which they harangued the crowds with considerable skill and effect; most, however, preferred to visit one family at a time, dealing with the health and financial problems large families bring, the heightened enjoyment of marital sex when the fear of conception is removed, the compensatory payment of Rs 30, the trivial nature of the operation, and so on. Over a period of time, most of the canvassers developed an articulate and effective "sales pitch." Some professed to be able to convince as many as half of the families they approached; for the majority, the average seems to be in the vicinity of 20 or 25 percent, but, of these, some would be rejected at the clinic because of ill health or other reasons.

The productivity of these operators varied considerably. Some, with widespread contacts and effective organisations, generated 100 to 200 cases in a month; others, operating mostly alone, managed to bring in 20 to 30. The average might have been 40 or 50 cases per month. These accounted for by far the majority of all vasectomies performed in Madras State. Despite a structure of social workers and health educators, virtually all operations in the city were promoted by canvassers;

in the rural areas, the panchayat organisations accounted for a fraction about 20 percent, of the cases. On this scale, the average monthly income of the canvasser might have been about Rs 200 to Rs 400 per month, depending on the amount of fee-splitting and working expenses. This is not very large but is still more than twice as high as the average incomes of labourers and lower-level clerks. This income has undoubtedly been the principal incentive, since canvassers generally were held in low esteem by most elements of the community. Most underwent petty harassment and extortion by the police, ridicule, and occasional verbal abuse as they worked in the villages. Primarily, it was the occupation which was looked down upon, rather than family planning or vasectomy itself. Canvassers tended to originate in lower-class and lower-caste communities and to work primarily among those communities. In this connection, it is interesting that a major interest among canvassers was in obtaining more overt support from the government in the form of official endorsement and publicity and marks of status like badges and uniforms—all of which would serve to raise their prestige.

This general description of the working of the vasectomy incentive programme in Madras State brings out several important features. First, it evoked extensive networks of informants and agents operating at grass-roots level outside the government bureaucratic structure; second, it created a fairly stable group of self-selected, successful entrepreneurs able to earn through performance alone much more than they could in other occupations open to them; third, this group was much closer, in terms of social distance, to the target population than the salaried government social worker, who identifies in dress, speech, and aspirations with the middle-class civil service; fourth, canvassers were markedly successful in reaching those disadvantaged segments of the community least accessible to the regular machinery and to mass media; fifth, the programme effectively enlisted the cooperation of "satisfied customers" as agents and informants of the canvassers; and sixth, it resulted in the intensive use of clinical facilities by drawing clients to them from a wide geographic area.

On the other hand, widespread criticism was directed at the use of significant monetary incentives for individual promoters in this and other family planning programmes. From discussions with doctors, psychologists, family planning officials and knowledgeable individuals in Madras and elsewhere, the major objections were discovered to be as follows: (1) the canvassers, in their zeal for cases, did not educate the fathers adequately and even may have misrepresented the nature of the operation; (2) they frequently neglected to obtain the consent of the wife and forged her signature on the written release; (3) they sometimes brought men who were bachelors, over age, or who had fewer than three living children; (4) they sometimes swindled the patient out of all or part of his compensatory grant of Rs 30; and (5) they were motivated solely by a pecuniary incentive rather than a concern for family welfare, and in some cases were realising exorbitant incomes. Such criticisms have caused family planning authorities in other parts of India to have official attitudes ranging from opposition through ambivalence to timidity. Some states were vehemently opposed on ethical grounds to "creating a class of touts in the family planning programme." In at least one state, greater use of such incentives had been prevented out of concern for the financial cost involved. In one neighbouring state, the Madras model was disliked primarily because of the malpractices listed above experienced by men recruited across the border by canvassers.

Five other states had up to 1965 adopted incentives to promoters in the vasectomy programme of Rs 2 and Rs 3. Recently, the Centre Government declared financial support for incentives of Rs 2 to promoters in sterilisation operations and Rs 1 for "neighbors and dais" (midwives) in loop insertions. Central support has been highly ambivalent, and such fees have been viewed as a temporary expedient to gain momentum and rather undesirable in themselves.

In Madras State itself, these criticisms of the canvasser programme led (after the initial three-year experimental period expired) to its temporary discontinuance, and, more recently, to another interruption. But, since this severely affected the number of vasectomy cases performed, the programme was later reinstated in a modified form, with better means of control over the activities of the canvassers. In short, fear of unethical practices and doubts about the propriety and long-term consequences of the programme have deterred other areas from emulating the Madras experience, despite its proven effectiveness in promoting vasectomy on a mass basis.

These judgements have not, however, been based on any reasoned analysis of the frequency or risk of malpractice or of the effectiveness of the canvasser programme in raising the case level. Information in other areas about the Madras experience rarely rises above the level of anecdote; nor has any serious attempt been made to attach social costs to the disadvantages of the scheme and to weigh these against the positive contributions. As a result, the latter have been implicitly grossly underestimated and the former much exaggerated. Owing to this lack of a systematic approach to decision-making, there has been little stimulus even to gather the relevant information, although much has been collected in the state simply for accounting purposes. Much of the rest of this study summarises an attempt to provide such a decision framework and to fill it in with what data are now available.

This implies, in first instance, some measure of the expected benefits of the canvasser programme. These have been interpreted as primarily economic, since family planning is really an economic programme in India. Assessment of these benefits requires consideration of three components: first, the economic consequences of a reduction of the birthrate; second, the impact of a vasectomy programme on the birthrate; third, the impact of canvasser activities on the vasectomy programme. The first component has been explored by such economists as Enke and Hoover.[8] In my study, a basically similar model using more recent data has been estimated, one which counts the costs of new births as the discounted resource cost of their consumption expenditure plus the social overhead capital outlay occasioned by them in such fields as housing, water supply and sanitation, and education; and which counts the economic contribution of new births as the discounted marginal product of their labour, taking into account labour force participations rates and the demographic characteristics of the population. This framework implies the assumption that the difference between these two magnitudes measures the additional resources available for consumption by those who are born and implies that no social value is placed on additional population in itself. Such a premise, as any social welfare assumption, may be contested, but for India at the present time, when realised family size is well above desired family size and the government is faced with the threat of faster population growth unless a major family planning programme succeeds, the assumption seems not too unrealistic. The only significant departure of this model from those cited above is in the attempt to explore the time-phasing of benefits from a reduction in the number of births.

This sketch will not satisfy the many questions which may arise in the mind of the interested reader, so a full description of the model and the data is given in the appendix to this chapter. The major qualifications to the empirical results which should be kept in mind are (a) that the model is a partial one which very incompletely encompasses the effects of population on the economy, and (b) that most of the forecasts are subject to a considerable range of error. However, the data have been treated as conservatively as possible; sensitivity analyses have been run on some of the key parameters; and the model and data have been presented in such a way as to facilitate substitutions or reworking.

At the 1966 estimated levels of average personal adult consumption and marginal value of labor services, Rs 400 and Rs 375 per annum respectively, the present value of 1000 births prevented in 1966 over a fifty-year time horizon with a 10 percent discount factor is in the vicinity of Rs 1,500,000 in constant 1960-61 prices. Of this, about Rs 300,000, or 20 percent, can be attributed to the first five years of the period, and about Rs 1,000,000, or two-thirds, to the first fifteen years. The total costs associated with the "first generation," the births directly prevented, account for almost 90 percent of the total. This indicates that, despite impressions to the contrary, birth preventions have a substantial impact on economic growth within a short time horizon of fifteen, ten, or even five years. In view of the average length of gestation lags and shakedown periods for major investments in industry, irrigation, and other capital projects, it is possible that the returns to birth prevention are at least as rapid.

The present value of 1000 births prevented in future years declines rapidly with time, as shown in Table 24 to Rs 900,000 for 1971 and Rs 550,000 in 1976. In large part this is explainable by the application of a 10 percent discount factor to the savings: resources saved in the present are considerably more valuable than those saved in the future. Demographic trends, such as falling mortality rates, increasing urbanisation, and altered age structure of the population, tend to work in both directions.

In Table 25 the present value of 1000 births prevented in successive years from 1966 is presented under two assumptions. The first has been discussed above. In the second, it is assumed that the present marginal product of adult male labour is not Rs 375 per annum but Rs 500. This 33 percent higher estimate reduces the present value of birth prevention by about 13 percent. This difference is minor relative to the decline in the value of birth prevention with time.

The figures in Table 25 have been derived on the assumption that present levels of per capita consumption and marginal product remain unchanged. This is scarcely tenable. As explained in the appendix to this chapter, however, it is more reasonable to suppose that over long periods of time the average annual rate of growth of per capita consumption will closely resemble that of the per capita marginal product of labour. Under this second approximating assumption, that these rates will be the same, results were obtained for rates of growth of 1 percent, the present value of 1000 births prevented in 1966 would be not Rs 1,500,000 but Rs 1,875,000; and at 2.5

TABLE 25. Present Value of One Thousand Births Prevented in Each of Successive Years at 1960-61 Prices and under Alternative Estimates of Value of Marginal Value of Labour to the Economy[a]

Year of prevention	Marginal product of labour per year	
	Rs 375	Rs 500
1966	1,500,000	1,300,000
1967	1,350,000	1,200,000
1968	1,200,000	1,050,000
1969	1,100,000	950,000
1970	1,000,000	850,000
1971	900,000	775,000
1972	800,000	700,000
1973	725,000	625,000
1974	650,000	575,000
1975	600,000	525,000
1976	550,000	475,000
1977	475,000	425,000
1978	425,000	375,000
1979	400,000	350,000
1980	350,000	300,000
1981	325,000	275,000

[a]Figures have been rounded to the nearest 25,000.

percent, Rs 2,425,000. These are significant differences and indicate the greater importance of population control in countries in which the "demonstration effect" and rising demands for social services exert upward pressure on consumption standards.

The second component of the analysis of benefits is the impact of vasectomy on birth prevention. This will depend primarily on the age distribution of the men who have undergone vasectomy and of their wives, the age-specific fertility rates of the latter, and the mortality rates of couples. In the

TABLE 26. Expected Number of Births Prevented in Subsequent
Years per Thousand Vasectomies or IUD Insertions

Year after operation	Births prevented by vasectomy[a]	Births prevented by IUD insertion
0	0	0
1	277	375
2	191	150
3	191	125
4	191	50
5	191	50
6	191	0
7	117	0
8	117	0
9	117	
10	117	
11	117	
12	48	
13	48	
14	48	
15	48	

[a]The total number of births prevented by vasectomy is expected to be about 2,500. The table above truncates about 5 percent of these over the last 10 years not included in the interval.

appendix to this chapter, estimates have been developed of the expected number of births prevented in each subsequent year per 1000 vasectomy operations performed in the current year. Analogous calculations were also made for IUD insertions. Data and assumptions are fully explained there. It is interesting that vasectomies in Madras seem to have a substantially *higher* birth-preventing effect than do those performed elsewhere in India. The reason is, contrary to current impressions, that the age distribution of the husbands and wives undergoing sterilisation is weighted with younger people. In a mass programme, families with large numbers of children are likely to be reached

TABLE 27. Present Value of Vasectomies[a] and IUD Insertions per Thousand, with Alternate Estimates of Labour Product and Annual Growth Rates of Per Capita Consumption and Product[b]

(Thousands of Rupees)

	Marginal product equals Rs 375			Marginal product equals Rs 500		
Year	Growth rate, in percent per annum					
	0	1	2.5	0	1	2.5
Vasectomy						
1966	1750	2350	3250	1525	2050	2825
1967	1575	2125	2975	1375	1850	2600
1968	1425	1950	2750	1250	1675	2400
1969	1275	1775	2550	1125	1525	2225
1970	1150	1625	2400	1000	1400	2075
1971	1050	1475	2250	900	1300	1950
1972	950	1350	2125	825	1200	1825
1973	875	1250	2000	750	1125	1725
1974	800	1150	1900	700	1050	1600
1975	725	1050	1800	650	975	1525
IUD insertion						
1966	900	1200	1625	800	1000	1325
1967	825	1100	1500	725	925	1250
1968	750	1000	1400	650	850	1150
1969	675	925	1300	575	775	1075
1970	600	850	1200	525	700	1000
1971	550	775	1125	475	650	925
1972	500	700	1050	425	600	850
1973	450	650	950	400	550	800
1974	400	600	875	350	500	750
1975	350	550	825	325	450	700

[a]The data used in the calculations for the benefits of vasectomy are relevant more to Madras State than to the nation as a whole. See appendix to this chapter for details.
[b]Figures rounded to nearest 25,000.

first; in Madras these families have already been contacted to a large extent, and the canvassers have been apparently pushing into a younger stratum of families with fewer children. Table 26 presents the expected number of births per 1000 vasectomies in each subsequent year, based on parameters most relevant to Madras. The underlying distributions are grouped into five-year intervals, which explains the stepped form of the unsmoothed estimates. Table 26 also presents the most plausible estimate of the number of births prevented per 1000 IUD insertions, as explained in the appendix.

With the information above on the first two components of the estimated benefits, the economic savings per 1000 vasectomies and IUD insertions have been estimated for each year from 1966 to 1975, in terms of the present value to the economy. Table 27 presents these results. Under the preferred assumption that labour is worth Rs 375 per adult man-year at the margin, the present value of 1000 vasectomies in 1966 seems to be at least Rs 1,750,000, and that of 1000 IUD insertions Rs 900,000. The former value is greater because vasectomies prevent more births, although over a longer period of time.

These estimates point up the value of time in family planning programmes, and it is instructive to evaluate the cost of lags in goal fulfillment in these terms. The tentative Fourth Plan national targets for IUD insertion and sterilisation are shown in the tabulation below.[9]

Year	IUD (millions)	Sterilisation (millions)
1966/67	1.80	0.38
1967/68	2.30	0.52
1968/69	3.50	0.67
1969/70	5.40	0.82
1970/71	6.00	1.12

TABLE 28. Chronology of the Canvasser Programme in Madras

Date	Event
1956	Official adoption of sterilisation programme; start of Rs 30 compensatory payment adopters
November 1959	Start of Rs 10 payment to canvassers in Madras City and to panchayat organisations in rural areas
April 1963	Abolition of payments to promoters of sterilisation cases
September 1963	Restoration of a payment (Rs 3) to canvassers
January 1964	Introduction of primary health centres into the sterilisation programme
August 1964	Introduction of a modified canvasser system, involving payment of Rs 10 to canvassers and to panchayats; canvassers attached to Madras City clinics were restricted to urban areas; canvassers were also attached to district hospitals and could work with primary health centres
August 1965	Canvassers attached to Madras City hospitals were no longer restricted to urban areas

Although sterilisation includes targets for both male and female sterilisations, the figures derived for male sterilisation alone can be applied without hesitation, since sterilisation of females would have at least as great birth-preventive effect.

Taking the lower valuation of labour and the most conservative estimate of growth rates, the present value of such an achievement would be no less than Rs 1836 crores. If this figure seems remarkably high, it should be remembered that a family planning programme of this dimension would prevent more than 20 million births, which is more than the total

TABLE 29. Time Series Data on Vasectomies Performed in Madras

Date	Madras City clinics	District hospitals	Primary health centres
1956	5	20	—
1957	76	155	—
1958	325	661	—
1959	436	894	—
1960	2,148	3,036	—
1961	11,202	11,218	—
1962	25,574	20,890	—
1963–I	7,662	—	—
II			—
III }	2,089	14,253	—
IV	—	—	—
1964–I	600	2,417	540
II	1,036	2,412	587
III	2,641	3,418	610
IV	2,493	8,588	2,000
1965–I	1,118	5,548	1,838
II	1,542	8,067	3,912
III	1,990	17,123	8,751
IV	3,219	36,870	20,931
1966–I	2,841	24,524	10,388
II	5,374	25,219	17,844
III	8,108	37,207	39,743

Source: Office of the Madras State Family Planning Officer.

populations of the large majority of countries in the world. If the programme should lag just one year, with IUD insertions in 1966 limited to one million and sterilisations to 0.2 million, then the present value of economic loss over the Fourth Plan period would be more than Rs 400 crores, in terms of savings foregone.

To complete the estimate of benefits, all that is now needed is a measure of the impact of canvasser activities on the scale of the vasectomy programme. Fortunately for this exercise, the Madras government within the period 1959-1966 began the use of promoters' fees, abolished them, reinstated them at a lower rate, and then restored the original sum while extending the coverage to all clinical facilities in the state. This provides sufficient variation in the "independent variable" to permit some investigation of the response.

Table 28 presents a brief chronology of these changes, and the available data on the number of vasectomies performed during these years are set forth in Table 29. It is apparent that abolition of the incentive scheme resulted in an abrupt decline in the number of operations performed and that restoration of the canvasser programme and its extension to district hospitals and primary health centres were followed by a marked increase in the pace of vasectomy.

A somewhat more formal statistical analysis bears out this association. Using annual data, the number of vasectomies was regressed on three variables: the incentive paid to promoters (F), a dummy variable (D), and a linear time trend (T). Regressions were run separately for city hospitals, district hospitals, and then for all Madras State, because, as Table 27 indicates, there were differences in timing and substance of the programme in the two former and in the primary health centres. For the city hospitals, the dummy variable distinguishes those periods during which canvassers were restricted to the metropolitan area and were not permitted to recruit cases from the countryside. For the district hospitals, the dummy variable represents that period during which incentive payments were offered to *individual* promoters as well as to the village panchayat organisations, marking the extension of the canvasser system to these clinics. For all Madras, the dummy should be given the same interpretaion, but with the complication that this period coincides with the entrance of new clinical facilities in primary

149

health centres to the vasectomy programme. Because annual data were used, it was necessary to weight the size of the incentive fee by the fraction of the year during which it was in effect; for example, a Rs 10 fee offered during half of a year is treated as a fee of Rs 5 in effect for the whole year. The results are as follows: [10]

A) City hospitals

$$V = -4352 + 675F - 9290D + 1645T \quad R^2=0.68 \quad \bar{R}^2=0.50$$
$$(0.13) \quad (0.08) \quad (0.06)$$

B) District hospitals

$$V = -12799 + 1521F + 38362D + 2891T \quad R^2=0.70 \quad \bar{R}^2=0.52$$
$$(0.26) \quad (0.10) \quad (0.28)$$

C) All Madras State

$$V = -26618 + 2471F + 62748D + 6451T \quad R^2=0.64 \quad \bar{R}^2=0.44$$
$$(0.31) \quad (0.15) \quad (0.27)$$

These regressions seek to measure the additional vasectomies associated with the canvasser programme over and above the trend increase due to increased clinical facilities, the impact of extension education and other publicity, and the generally rising levels of education and awareness of family planning. (In view of the substantial negative intercepts, it is probable that the trend could better be expressed by an exponential or other nonlinear relationship.)

While the fee variable (F) is not very significant except in the Madras City hospital case, the overall results—taking into consideration the dummy variables—support the contention that the canvasser programme has had a substantial impact. These dummy variables, especially in relation to A) and B), also represent the operation of the programme, and are both significant and quantitatively important. That in equation B) can be entirely associated with the extension of the system to rural areas. Although that in equation C) reflects to some extent the increase in clinical facilities in primary health centres, it is also plausible to take one-half of the increment (i.e., ½ (62748–38362)) as also attributable to the work of the canvassers. Canvassers prefer to take patients to the primary health centres in rural areas because it is geographically more convenient than to go to district headquarters, because the local person feels more at ease in smaller, less crowded, and more familiar clinics, and because the doctors and assistants there are less likely to subject the prospect to a detailed interview and examination.

This establishes some measure, albeit a crude one, of the impact of the canvasser programme. From the relation for all Madras, substituting F = Rs 10, it appears that the total quantitative effect was about 75,000 additional cases per year; this is little more than 25 percent of the total number of vasectomies at the 1966 rate. The conservative nature of this estimate can be clearly seen from the fact that, were these cases eliminated, Madras would still have been operating at a higher per capita rate than any other state in India.

The quality of the basic data did not permit investigation of the lag relation between changes in the canvasser programme and the response of the vasectomy rate, although the crude figure suggests some lag effect exists. Therefore, if these 75,000 vasectomies per year are valued at the current, conservative estimate of Rs 1,750,000 per thousand as in Table 37, the annual benefits from the programme are estimated at Rs 13.1 crores. *The present value of the programme over the next five years would be more than Rs 53 crores!* This corresponds to an expected total prevention of births from these vasectomies of over 900,000.

In considering the benefits of the canvasser system, one other factor should be kept in mind. Overwhelmingly, the greater number of men recruited by canvassers have come from the lower economic strata, the least educated, the least aware of family planning techniques, the most burdened by large families, and the least accessible through more conventional means of promotion and publicity. The best available data on the economic status of men undergoing vasectomy are found in an unpublished follow-up study by Dr. P. G. Krishnan covering 1,000 patients operated on during 1958 and until 1965 at the government Royahpettah Hospital in Madras City. Krishnan gives the following distribution of patients according to monthly income:

Income group	No. of patients	Percentage
up to Rs 50	571	57.1
Rs 51-Rs 100	390	39.0
Rs 101-Rs 150	29	2.9
Rs 151 and up	10	1.0

It is striking that full 96 percent of these men reported income of less than Rs 100 per month. Even allowing for underreporting and the difficulty in estimating income from Indian farming, the lower-class preponderance is beyond dispute. Similarly, almost 45 percent of the sample were illiterate and 71 percent had less than six years of schooling, as shown in the tabulation below:

Educational level	No. of cases	Percentage
Illiterate	447	44.7
1st-5th standard	263	26.3
6th-8th standard	218	21.8
Up to high school	72	7.2
High school graduate	0	0

Against these benefits, the direct financial costs are small. The relevant costs are incremental costs. In most states, some clinical facilities for vasectomy and an administrative structure have already been installed or will be installed whether incentives are adopted or not. These facilities are now considerably underutilised. In Madras it is clear that at least some of the facilities, especially those in Madras City, have been created in response to the demands generated by the incentive programme and therefore can be reasonably considered incremental. To forestall controversy, *all* the operating expenses of the vasectomy programme have been charged on the cost side in this calculation. This is a gross overestimate, since most of the facilities in rural areas would have been created anyway and since many of the personnel are involved in other family planning, family welfare, and medical activities.

Allowance has been made for four city hospitals of the costs of two full-time units, thirty-seven district clinics with full-time units, and 137 primary health centres with part-time units. The estimated total cost of these facilities has been charged to the programme, exclusive of buildings, furnishings, and similar overheads. Estimates are based on centrally-sanctioned staffing patterns for the extended family planning programme. The objective has been not to obtain the most accurate figure possible but to estimate an upper bound to the range of reasonable possibilities, so generous contingency factors were added at all stages. Table 30 gives summary data, and the detailed figures are given in the appendix to this chapter.

The result is that even under the most generous estimate, the annual cost of the programme cannot exceed Rs 2.5 crores. Therefore, on a straight economic calculation the benefit-cost ratio of the incentive programme is at least five to one, and probably much greater than that. The net benefit of the

TABLE 30. Estimated Total Costs for Vasectomy with Incentive Scheme[a]

Cost category	Rate	Total cost
Clinical costs		
PHC's	137 at Rs 20,000/year	27,40,000
District	37 at Rs 30,000/year	11,10,000
City	4 at Rs 34,000/year	1,36,000
Administrative costs		
District level	12 at Rs 28,000/year	3,36,000
State level		54,000
Contingency factor	100% of Total	43,76,000
		87,52,000
Incentives to patients and canvassers		
Urban cases	20,000 at Rs 40/year	8,00,000
Rural cases	200,000 at Rs 60/year	1,20,00,000
		1,28,00,000
Incentives to doctors		
City hospitals		32,000
Elsewhere		37,000
		2,16,19,000

[a]Dr. Howard Mitchell of the Ford Foundation in India has kindly supplied the underlying data on staffing patterns and salary levels. Unit costs refer implicitly to the year 1965-66.

programme is at least Rs 10.6 crores, or Rs 1413 per vasectomy attributable to it, in terms of present value.

The next step is to estimate the intangible costs of the programme. Indeed, it is in this area that the most serious objections have been raised, based largely on rumoured or reported "malpractices." Two steps are involved: first, to estimate the frequency of these "abuses" with available historical data;

TABLE 31. Age Distribution of Vasectomy Patients and Number
of Living Children, Madras Follow-up Survey

Age, years	Number	Percent	Number of children	Number	Percent
15-20			0	18	1.8
21-25	24	2.4	1	35	3.5
26-30	141	14.1	2	141	14.1
31-35	275	27.3	3	488	48.8
36-40	233	23.3	4	192	19.1
41-45	253	25.3	5	76	7.6
46-50	63	6.3	6	13	1.3
51-55	5	0.5	7 and up	5	0.5

second, to assign a weight to them. Of course, these intangible
costs stem basically from some contravention of government
policy defining the desirable operation of the system. In Madras,
the key provisions are, to repeat, that (a) the patient should be
a healthy married man under fifty years of age with three
living children, (b) he should be fully aware of the nature of
the operation and consent in the light of its implications, and
(c) his wife should also give her consent in writing.

The basic data on the frequency of contraventions of these
provisions stem from the follow-up survey cited previously
and from a survey of 1183 patients residing in Kolar District
in Mysore State who had undergone vasectomy in Madras. The
latter study was carried out under the direction of the Deputy
Director of Health Services (Family Planning) in the government of Mysore (see Tables 31 and 32).

According to the Mysore study, which is by far the less
favourable, 28.5 percent of the men who underwent vasectomy
had fewer than three children, 17.6 percent were fifty years of

TABLE 32. Age Distribution of Vasectomy Patients and Number of Children; Mysore Study

Age, years	Number	Percent	Less than three children	Number of children	Number	Percent
20-24	6	0.5	5	0	78	6.6
25-29	62	5.2	42	1	92	7.7
30-34	215	19.2	98	2	168	14.2
35-39	260	22.0	71	3	230	19.4
40-44	266	22.5	45	4	222	18.8
45-49	166	14.0	27	5	172	14.5
50-54	119	10.1	23	6	113	9.6
55-59	35	3.0	13	7	32	2.7
60-64	41	3.5	8	8	30	2.5
64-69	6	0.5	2	9	17	1.4
70 plus	5	0.4	4	10 plus	6	0.5
no data	2	0.2		no data	3	0.3
	1183	100.0	338		1183	100.0

Number of patients not married: 23 (2 percent)
Number of patients widowed: 13 (1 percent)
Number of complications: 45 (4 percent)

age or more, and 4.4 percent were in both categories. In the Madras survey it appeared that 18 percent of the men had fewer than three children and that only one percent were over fifty. There are considerable differences between these estimates, perhaps owing in part to the fact that screening tends to be more rigourous in Madras City than in the rural areas where the Mysore patients had been brought. One problem common to both studies is that it was not made clear whether the date of referral was the date of the operation or the date on which the survey was carried out. If the latter, the age distributions would be shifted up and the distribution of numbers of living children would be shifted down through mortality.

On other violations of policy, there is less empirical evidence.
In interviews with family planning workers and canvassers, it
was estimated that about 25 percent of all the wives' signatures
were forgeries. This is naturally a difficult estimate to verify.
It is equally difficult to speculate on the percentage of men
who were ill-informed or misinformed about the operation. One
bit of evidence that can be cited is the fact that about 5 percent of the men brought to hospital in Madras City "abscond"
before the operation can be performed—clear evidence of a
certain lack of preparation. Others are undoubtedly equally
unprepared but too cowed or unsuspecting to retreat. On the
other hand, most of those who give way to apprehension are
followed up by the field worker and eventually return to undergo the operation. All in all, a figure of 5 percent for the ill-
informed is not implausible.

In summary, it appears from what evidence there is at present
that contraventions of the existing policy of the Madras government have been significant. Although this evidence can only be
regarded as tentative, it would not be out of keeping with the
data to assume that in roughly 50 percent of the cases, some
aspect of official policy is violated, the most frequent contraventions being those related to the number of children of the
patient and the signature of the patient's wife. For this reason,
it is necessary to consider more carefully the weight of these
intangible costs. On a conceptual level, the previous arguments
lead to the conclusion that if *no* social value is attached to such
cases and credit is taken only for half the additional cases, the net
social benefit from the programme is still at least three to one. If
a *negative* social value, or social cost, is attached, then it is possible to conclude that the total social costs can outweigh the
benefits.

The implications of this finding need to be carefully considered. Of course, it is the responsibility of the officials in charge

of the programme to make, explicitly or implicitly, the value judgments underlying policy. However, the very fact that a large percentage of the men *have chosen* vasectomy, even though having only one or two living children, suggests a significant divergence between private and official judgments in this area. This is not surprising in view of the enormous gap in class, caste, training, circumstances, and outlook between those who set family planning policy and those who are the beneficiaries of the vasectomy programme. The important factor would seem to be that in coming to a decision the family should have the full facts and implications of the alternatives before them. This of course includes knowledge of alternative nonpermanent methods of contraception.

More fundamentally, however, it can be argued that the relevant and appropriate weight of these intangible costs is the actual incremental cost of eliminating them. These additional costs can be shown to be insignificant in comparison to the benefits of the programme. For example, a major concern has been that canvassers, either because of their financial interest or because of their limited educational background, may often do an inadequate job of educating the patient and explaining the nature of the operation. This danger can be eliminated by stationing a health education officer at each clinic to talk to each group of patients before their operations. At present, this is being done to greater or lesser degrees in various hospitals in Madras, depending largely on the procedures adopted by the individual institutions. The personnel are already in place in the form of health education officers at block and district levels. However, even assuming an additional full-time officer at each of the 180 clinics, at an annual pay of Rs 3600 per annum, only Rs 6.48 lakhs would be added to programme costs.

Similarly, the problems of restricting the programme to eligible couples, however defined, can be solved at relatively minor cost. One of the problems to be overcome is the mobility of the canvassers and the prospective vasectomy patients: the city hospitals accept significant numbers of cases from over a hundred miles away and even from other states. However, one of the functions of the health education and family planning extension staff at present is to draw up, from surveys and from registers of births maintained in each village, a current list of eligible couples. To carry out this work more thoroughly in rural areas might require additional personnel at the block level: say, a statistical officer at Rs 3000 per annum and a clerical assistant at Rs 2000, in each of the approximately 300 blocks in the state. This would add about Rs 15 lakhs to programme costs. In urban areas, the same staff might be provided for each 50,000 of population. With an urban population of roughly 7 million, this would imply 140 more teams and a further cost of Rs 7 lakhs per annum. With a contingency factor of Rs 3 lakhs, one can safely conclude that the problem of determining the eligible couples might be solved at an annual cost of about Rs 25 lakhs.

The other part of the problem, however, is to identify these eligible individuals when they appear at the clinic. The most practical solution suggested to date is to entrust the panchayat president or other local, disinterested official, with the task of issuing to eligible couples desiring vasectomy for the husband an identity card to be presented at the clinic. This card would be signed by the panchayat president and stamped with an official seal, and it would contain a description of the individual and a certification of the relevant facts. Since it is a typical procedure for the canvasser to involve the panchayat officials in his work in any case, by approaching them for support in the village and for the names of poor families with numerous children, this scheme would not necessitate a large departure from existing procedures. It would also virtually solve the problem in rural areas, since most canvassers operate in a radius of fifteen or twenty miles of their home base most of the time, and each clinic, if necessary, could be furnished with a specimen signature from each panchayat president in his vicinity. This scheme could be carried out at a cost not exceeding a few lakhs, say Rs 5 lakhs per year, and yield effective control over the recipient group in the vasectomy programme.

In summary, the total cost of the preventive measures outlined above on a generous estimation would amount to only Rs 36 lakhs per annum. Apportioned over the 75,000 incremental vasectomies, this would amount to only Rs 50 per case. If this be accepted as the true cost of these "intangible factors," as it should be, then it is obvious that the canvasser programme should not be prejudiced on their account. To put it another way, since the annual net social benefits of the programme have been close to Rs 13 crores, there is an enormous margin left to finance whatever additional steps are deemed necessary to make it run more smoothly. The weight of this argument can be seen from the fact that even if it were necessary to *double* the outlay on the programme, it would be worthwhile to do so.

The foregoing pages have attempted to demonstrate, first of all, the value of an explicit decision-making framework in programmes surrounded with risk and uncertainty, if for no other reason than to stimulate a closer definition of policy weights and to provide a focus and incentive for the application of data to the decision process. If this is done, even crude information subject to a considerable range of error often suffices to determine the correct policy. In this example, the benefits from the programme—or any programme that is effective in accelerating the progress of population control—are so high that a strong presumption is created in its favour. This is the underlying rationale for the government of India's willingness to under-write "all that can usefully be spent." This kind of analysis, in which the benefits are constantly in view, can lead to more forceful and expeditious decision making.

This case study also demonstrates the important role that private initiatives and organisation can play in forwarding a pro-gramme when administrative structure and personnel are a real constraint. A relatively small incentive resulted in a remarkably extensive and complex system which generated information on the identity of potential candidates for vasectomy; brought to bear an intensive effort at persuasion; provided services like transportation, food, lodging, and guidance to the prospective patient; and effectively enlisted the subsequent active support of men who had undergone vasectomy in persuading others. Such private initiative and administrative effort are not substitutes, but complements. In this example, canvassers and their agents were able to reach into the villages and their households to pro-vide an effective personal contact; this is something the "exten-sion" structure cannot do as well. On the other hand, general education and publicity, enlistment of support among local leaders, and overall direction and control over the programme are functions of the administration, and the canvassers themselves have realised their dependence on the family planning structure for a favourable environment in which to work.

Of course, the canvasser programme was but one small aspect of the Indian family planning effort, and this study is not in-tended to exaggerate its importance. It is but a part of the overall range of incentives: to doctors, voluntary organisations and local bodies, and "adopters," as well as to promoters. Many

TABLE 33. Incentives in Sterilisation Programmes in 1965-1966 by States

| State | Sterilisations per thousand of population | Incentives, rupees per case | | | | | |
		Male	Female	Local Body	Promoter	Doctor Government	Private
Madras	3.42	30	30	10	10	a	5
Orissa	2.61	13	18	–	3	–	10[b]
Kerala	2.30	17	20	–	2	3	10
Maharashthra	1.49	10	10	5[b]	–	3.5[b]	3.5[b]
Punjab	1.43	10	10	–	2	–	–
Mysore	1.00	5	5	3	–	2.5[b]	10
Uttar Pradesh	0.94	10	10	–	2	4	–
Gujerat	0.86	15	25	–	2	–	–
Andhra Pradesh	0.73	10	10	10[b]	–	–	10[b]
Madhya Pradesh	0.72	–	–	–	–	–	–
West Bengal	0.48	10	10	–	–	–	–
Assam	0.44	–	–	–	–	–	–
Rajasthan	0.42	–	–	–	–	–	–
Jammu, Kashmir	0.38	–	–	–	–	–	–
Bihar	0.05	25	25	–	–	–	–

Sources: Sterilisations per capita: Central Family Planning Council, Agenda Notes, Enclosure 3 (p). Incentives: Planning Commission, Programme Evaluation Organisation, *Evaluation of the Family Planning Programme* (Delhi, 1965), p. 81ff. U.N. Advisory Mission, *Report on the Family Planning Program in India.*

[a]Special allowance of Rs 50 for a minimum of 30 cases per months, plus Rs 3 per case thereafter; for full-time doctors in city clinics, Rs 300 for 200 cases plus Rs 5 per case thereafter.

[b]For vasectomy "camps."

states have made use of such incentives, and most have found them to have some positive impact. Table 33 presents an interesting comparison of the incentives in force during 1965-66 for sterilisation programmes in the various states, arrayed in order of the number of cases per capita in that year. The relative position of Madras state is striking. Also, the association of relatively high performance with liberal use of monetary incentives, especially to promoters, is apparent. Mysore and Maharashtra, the two states in the upper half of the list which do not use promoters, have succeeded through a well-organised and energetic use of "camps." These data support the idea that incentives of various kinds can effectively complement administrative efforts. The Government of India has recently been moving to increase gradually the role of such incentives. In the vasectomy programme, it has sanctioned payments to patient, doctor, and promoter of Rs 17, 3 and 2 respectively. In the IUD programme, it has accepted levels of Rs 5, 2, and 1. The experience of Madras suggests that further incentives to promoters would strongly stimulate results in the short term, if suitable safeguards and controls were also adopted to ensure proper practices.

Appendix to Chapter 5

Data and Assumptions Underlying the Calculation of Present Values of Birth Prevention

I. THE SPECIFICATION OF THE MODEL

Broadly speaking, the conceptual framework used in the calculations are similar to those employed by Enke, Coale and Hoover, and others.[1] The model employed differs in several particulars, however, and these can best be explained with all the variables and relationships in full sight.

A. Variables

The variables that entered the calculations are identified in this section. The data used to measure them are discussed in the next section.

V_i = the present value of 1000 births prevented in year i.

r = a time discount rate used to discount future costs and benefits

i,j,k,t = subscripts denoting time, in years.

---

1. S. Enke, "The Gains to India from Population Control," *Review of Economics and Statistics,* 62 (May 1960) 175; "The Economics of Population Control," *Economic Journal,* 76 (March 1966) 44; A. J. Coale and E. M. Hoover, *Population Growth and Economic Development in Low-Income Countries* (Princeton, N.J., Princeton University Press, 1958).

$S_{i,j-i} =$ the number of survivors in year j-i per 1000 persons born in year i.

$C =$ the average annual personal consumption expenditure per 1000 adults in year 1 (Year 1= 1965/66), expressed in 1960/61 prices.

$F_{t-i} =$ the average annual personal consumption expenditure per 1000 persons t-i years of age, expressed as a fraction of the average annual personal consumption expenditure per 100 adults.

$G_{t-i} =$ the average annual outlay on education, housing, water supply, and sanitation attributable to 1000 people t-i years of age, in year t, expressed in 1960/61 prices.

$H_{t-i} =$ the average participation rate in the labour force of 1000 persons t-i years of age in year t.

$P =$ the marginal product of 1000 unskilled labourers to the economy in year 1, 1960/61 prices.

$B_{t-i} =$ the number of children born in year t to 1000 persons t-i years of age

With these variables in mind, the conceptual framework can first be written as follows, and then explained:

$$
V_i = \sum_{t=i}^{t=50} \Big\{ S_{i,t-i} (F_{t-i} C + G_{t-i} - H_{t-i} P) + \ldots
$$

$$
+ \sum_{j=i}^{j=t} \Big[S_{i,j-i} B_{j-i} S_{j,t-j} (F_{t-j} C + G_{t-j} - H_{t-j} P) + \ldots
$$

$$
+ \sum_{k=j}^{k=t} S_{j,k-j} B_{k-j} S_{k,t-k} (F_{t-k} C + G_{t-k} - H_{t-k} P) \qquad (1+r)^{-t}
$$

$$
i=1, \ldots, 16
$$

In effect, this formula states that the present value of 1000 births prevented in year i is the discounted sum of the annual net costs of the first generation plus the annual net costs of the second generation plus the annual net costs of the third generation. In any year, the net costs associated with the *survivors* of 1000 persons born in year i are taken to be the difference between the expenditure on personal consumption and the specified social services and the value of the productive services rendered by those persons.

For example, according to the first line of the formula, in the year t' there would be $S_{i,t'-i}$ survivors per 100 born in year i. The consumption attributable to that 1000 would have been $F_{t'-i} C + G_{t'-i}$, while the value of the marginal product would have been $H_{t'-i} P$. The product of the net cost times the survivorship ratio gives the costs of the first generation in year t'.

The second line asserts that in the same year there will be additional net costs associated with the survivors of the children born in each year from i to t' to the surviving members of the first generation.

The third line asserts that there will be similar costs associated with the surviving children of the second generation. To the children of the first generation born in each year j, there will be a certain number of children born in each year k from j to t', and these surviving children's consumption and production are taken into account.

This explicit statement of the model brings out certain of the underlying assumptions, which are restated verbally below:

1. The conceptual measure of personal and social consumption expenditure employed in this study is the *average* level of consumption per 1000. That is, it is assumed that the expenditures of additional persons will be determined by the stations in society into which they are born, which will determine the kinds of jobs, training, and incomes they will enjoy. On the other hand, the conceptual measure of the value of the product of additional persons in the labour force is the *marginal product* of labour, net of the effects of investment in human resources. These two conceptual measures are not inconsistent; to the extent that persons are born into higher socioeconomic milieus, they gain access to more training and more productive work. Their expenditure standards are thus determined, but the value of their labour must be taken net of the effects of status and training. The effects of status are fortuitous and represent merely a displacement of individuals within the economy. The effects of training are not fortuitous, but the returns to investment in human resources. Such investment at the margin can be assumed to just balance the stream of returns discounted at the social rate of interest, so that neither the investment costs nor the resulting product need be taken

into consideration. The *disposition* of the resulting product, however, in personal consumption by the income recipients is a real resource cost to the economy. Therefore, it is appropriate to use the average pattern of consumption together with the marginal product of labour.

There has been a great deal of discussion about the appropriate measure of labour's marginal product in India, in which much complete and partial unemployment is apparent. The above discussion leads to the conclusion that the marginal product of unskilled labour is relevant for this study. Further, in accordance with the reasoning of such economists as W. A. Lewis and Ranis and Fei, it is apparent that with 80 percent of the labour force deployed in agriculture, and a perfectly elastic supply of unskilled labour to the small industrial sector at the going wage (which may be above the marginal product in agriculture because of some immobility), the productivity of labour in agriculture is the appropriate conceptual measure. Although this conclusion seems to lead straight to the heart of the "disguised unemployment" controversy, it can be argued that a straightforward calculation of the average annual earnings of hired agricultural labour provides a conceptually sound and empirically accurate measure of the value of the marginal labour product in India. Since the multitude of private farm employers certainly do not hire labour as a social service and generally have available other sources of labour within their own families and caste groups, there is no reason to suppose that the earnings of hired labour are systematically higher than the value of the marginal product. On the other hand, it has been estimated that 43 percent of the agricultural labour households hold some land. Land is also available under various tenancy arrangements, and men workers are self-employed for a significant fraction of the year.[2] Therefore, there tend to be alternative avenues of employment of agricultural labour, and well-defined opportunity costs. This suggests the suppostion that the earnings of hired labour cannot systematically be exceeded by the value of the marginal product. If this is true, then there seems no reason not to accept these levels of earning as a valid measure of the marginal product. According to the Agricultural Labour Enquiry Report;[3] "The crux of such wage

2. Government of India, Ministry of Labour, *Report on the Second Enquiry into Agricultural Labour in India* (Delhi, 1960), p. 61.

3. Ibid., p. 63.

employment from the point of view of the landholder is the necessity to hire workers and his capacity to pay them. He will naturally employ only such numbers of labourers for such minimum periods as is absolutely necessary for getting the agricultural operations done . . . Before they think of employing hired labour, marginal cultivators make every effort to economise by intensive utilisation of family labour and by exhausting the scope for mutual help."

2. Both the average annual personal consumption per 1000, the value of the marginal product of labour, and the average per capita expenditure on social facilities are assumed to be constant over time. This assumption has been made for computational rather than intrinsic reasons. Reexamination of the calculating model will show that if these three variables C, P, and G_{t-i} grow at the same average annual rate, this rate can be factored out and incorporated into the discount rate r. That is, under this assumption, if the constant average annual growth rate were c, then the discount factor could be written as $[(1 + c)/(1 + r)]^t$. It is much more arguable that, to a reasonable degree of approximation, per capita consumption and the productivity of labour on the margin will tend to increase at the same rate over a long period of time, if not in the short run. This is, in fact, the maintained assumption. A range of discount rates r has been programmed into the actual computations, so that the implications of alternative growth rates can be investigated.

3. The age pattern of personal consumption expenditure is constant over time. That is, F_{t-i} depends only on $t-i$, the age of the consumer.

4. Similarly, the average participation rate in the labour force is not expected to change over time. This average participation rate, as explained more fully below, is a weighted average of the participation rates for urban men, urban women, rural men, and rural women. Further, the rates have been adjusted for the relative earnings of men, women, and children under fifteen. Thus, one might expect that even if the individual participation rates should remain constant over time, the increasing urbanisation rates would cause a change in the weights. This is certainly true, since approximately 30 to 35 percent of the future population growth is expected to be in urban areas. However, the effects are mitigated by the fact that most of the differences in participation rates between urban and rural areas, for men at least, occur in the early life years, when rural boys are more likely to be in the labour force than urban. However, migration,

which is expected to account for the major part of the increase in urban population,[4] typically takes place when the migrant is in his twenties.[5] Therefore, to use the weights for the earlier period is to assume, in effect, that migrants will work like rural boys and then like urban men. As a consequence, the errors due to changes in the weights are not likely to be serious.

5. The birthrate per 1000 persons is assumed to depend only on the age of the persons. That is, the age-specific gross fertility rates are assumed to be constant over time. At first blush, this assumption seems scarcely compatible with the aims of the family planning programme itself. However, it can be justified for the purposes of this calculation, since the use of fertility rates in the estimates is relevant only for calculation of second and third generation effects, which enter only after a minimum lag of fifteen years. Therefore, the values of the age-specific fertility rates assumed are *projections* of an average future rate. It is thus assumed that these future rates will be attained, by implication, regardless of the decisions that are taken currently regarding the family planning programme. If this independence is not assumed, the present value of birth prevention in a sense depends on itself, in that the fewer children parents have, the fewer grandchildren they will have. However, the lower birthrates in the future are expected to be, the less valuable is birth prevention in the present. (In an extreme case, if it were thought that births would cease altogether after twenty years, the value of family planning presently would diminish greatly.)

6. The time horizon for the calculations has been taken at fifty years from the initial time period. This interval is in one sense too long, in that there is little basis for projecting many of the relevant variables that far ahead. It is also quite long enough in another sense, in that at a reasonable rate of time discount events in that distant future are of but slight importance to current decisions. And, it is sufficiently long for the final effects of one generation to manifest themselves fully and for the second generation to manifest themselves to a considerable extent. (The youngest

4. Kingsley Davis, "Urbanization in India: Past and Future," in *India's Urban Future,* ed. R. Turner (Berkeley, University of California Press, 1962).

5. D. Bogue and K. C. Zacharish, "Urbanization and Migration in India," in *India's Urban Future,* p. 42.

children of the first generation would be five years old at the end of the period and the oldest thirty-five, for parents born in the initial year.)

7. Unlike the earlier calculations of Enke, this model introduces no special provisions for the costs of sacrificing future investment as distinct from future consumption. It is assumed that, on the margin, the stream of returns from investment outlays, discounted at the social rate of interest, would just equal their social costs. Therefore, the resource costs of the consumption outlays of additional population are the same whether these resources would otherwise have been devoted to investment or to consumption.

By implication, the social welfare expenditures included under G are assumed to be in the nature of consumption outlays rather than productive investments. This could be contested for education and housing, which are usually thought to be largely in the nature of "investments in human resources." These considerations have been taken into account. For education, only the costs of primary education have been taken into account as a social charge; higher education has been omitted as a self-liquidating productive investment. This distinction is supported by official policies and estimates. Primary education is to be provided on a free and compulsory basis to all children between the ages of six and fourteen, as their constitutional right and as the requirement of citizenship. Further education is to be provided to the extent possible, in accordance with the manpower requirements of the economy, with respect to both the number of students trained and the areas of training. The views of the planning commission are relevant in this regard: "Whereas education up to the age of fourteen must be universal and justified in itself as a right and requirement of a citizen, education beyond this stage must be primarily a preparation for life's work. The structuring of education would be in close relationship to a broad manpower plan . . . which ensures that at completion of every stage of education there should be avenues of fruitful employment."[6] This is not to say strictly that primary education does not raise the quality of the labour force, not that increases in population will not, *ceteris paribus,* force the society to provide more facilities for higher education. Both are obviously true. However, since

6. Perspective Planning Division, Planning Commission, *Notes on the Perspective of Development in India: 1960-61 to 1975-76* (Delhi, 1964), p. 239.

any division must be made on largely arbitrary grounds, it seems better to adhere to official positions. In any case, errors in the two assumptions would work to offset each other, leading to no obvious bias. Housing has been taken as an item of durable personal consumption and the value of the housing service discounted to the point of construction. There may be some double-counting involved in this procedure, since *rental* outlays would be also included in the category of personal consumption expenditure. However, most housing, especially in rural areas, is owner-occupied. Moreover, as discussed below, an extremely conservative estimate of housing outlays has been adopted, which should largely compensate for any degree of double-counting.

II. THE DATA

The series used on the calculations are presented in Table 34; their derivation and the sources of data are discussed below.

1. *The social rate of interest* The value adopted for this parameter is 10 percent, which is currently the target rate for public sector investments. A good case can be made for a figure in this range,[7] although 12 percent would have been equally appropriate. For reasons explained above, the calculations have also been carried through using a lower rate of 5 percent.

2. *The age-pattern of personal consumption expenditure* Little empirical information is available to us on the relative consumption outlays of persons in different age groups, other things held constant. The basic unit for budget studies is the household. Therefore, it was necessary to make an unsupported assumption about the shape of this function, which appears as F in Table 34.

3. *The present annual average adult personal consumption outlay per thousand* Like all values used in the calculations, this has been derived in 1960/61 prices. The method employed was to estimate the average personal consumption outlay per capita and the age distribution of the population. Then, on the basis of the assumed age pattern of consumption spending, it was possible to estimate the average adult per capita consumption outlay. That is, letting C/P be per capita consumption, C_a be

7. A. Harberger, "Cost-Benefit Analysis and Economic Growth," *Economic Weekly,* 14 (February 1962), 203 ff.

TABLE 34. Parameters for the Computation of Birth Prevention Benefits

Age of Person	F	G	H	B	
0	0.100	0	0	0	R (1)
1	0.150	0	0	0	(0.05)
2	0.200	0	0	0	
3	0.250	0	0	0	
4	0.250	25,000	0	0	R (2)
5	0.375	25,000	0.038	0	(0.10)
6	0.375	45,000	0.038	0	
7	0.375	45,000	0.038	0	
8	0.375	45,000	0.038	0	P (1)
9	0.375	45,000	0.038	0	(375,000)
10	0.625	70,310	0.038	0	
11	0.625	70,310	0.038	0	
12	0.625	70,310	0.174	0	P (2)
13	0.625	70,310	0.174	0	(500,000)
14	0.625	25,310	0.174	0	
15	0.750	25,310	0.415	0.0359	
16	0.750	25,310	0.462	0.0359	C
17	0.750	25,310	0.462	0.0359	(400,000)
18	0.750	25,310	0.565	0.0359	
19	0.750	25,310	0.565	0.0359	
20	1.000	25,310	0.565	0.0933	
21	1.000	25,310	0.565	0.0933	
22	1.000	25,310	0.623	0.0933	
23	1.000	25,310	0.623	0.0933	
24	1.000	25,310	0.623	0.0933	
25	1.000	25,310	0.623	0.1040	
26	1.000	25,310	0.623	0.1040	
27	1.000	25,310	0.656	0.1040	
28	1.000	25,310	0.656	0.1040	
29	1.000	25,310	0.656	0.1040	
30	1.000	0	0.656	0.0768	
31	1.000	0	0.656	0.0768	
32	1.000	0	0.656	0.0768	
33	1.000	0	0.656	0.0768	
34	1.000	0	0.656	0.0768	
35	1.000	0	0.656	0.0488	
36	1.000	0	0.656	0.0488	
37	1.000	0	0.656	0.0488	
38	1.000	0	0.659	0.0488	
39	1.000	0	0.659	0.0488	
40	1.000	0	0.659	0.0198	
41	1.000	0	0.659	0.0198	
42	1.000	0	0.659	0.0198	
43	1.000	0	0.659	0.0198	
44	1.000	0	0.659	0.0198	

TABLE 34. (continued)

Age of Person	F	G	H	B
45	1.000	0	0.659	0
46	1.000	0	0.659	0
47	1.000	0	0.563	0
48	1.000	0	0.563	0
49	1.000	0	0.563	0

per capita adult consumption, f_t be the consumption of a person t years of age as a fraction of adult consumption, and w_t be the fraction of the population t years of age, then

$$C/P = \sum_t (f_t w_t) \; C_a$$

Total personal consumption per capita in 1960/61 prices was derived from national income data. This yields an estimate of Rs 16,500 crores. It was assumed that the ratio of personal consumption to national income in 1965-66 was .88 compared to .93 for 1960-61. Current population was estimated to be 495 million, which results in a figure of about Rs 290 for per capita personal consumption.

The age distribution of the population in 1965-66 was taken to be the same as that for 1960-61. This was, according to census figures:[8]

0-4	16.2%	10-14	11.6%	20+	49.4%
5-9	13.6%	15-19	9.2%		

On this basis, the average per adult consumption outlay was estimated to be Rs 400 according to the formula presented above. This is presented in Table 1-A as Rs 400,000 per thousand.

4. *Expenditure on primary education, housing, water supply, and sanitation* For reasons explained above, only the costs of primary education were included. The capital costs per student have been estimated at Rs 50, assumed to be spread over two pre-enrollment years, and the current costs at Rs 45 per student over the years 6 to 14.[9]

Forecasts of the costs of urban and rural housing from the Perspective Planning Commission estimate that urban housing will cost Rs 1,000 per head in 1960-61 prices, including the cost of land and site preparation, over

8. Institute of Applied Manpower Research, *Factbook on Manpower* (Delhi, 1963), p. 13.

9. *Notes of Perspective of Development in India,* pp. 240, 241.

173

the Fourth and Fifth Plans.[10] This is admittedly a "modest" provision. For comparison, an earlier estimate was that urban housing, excluding the cost of land at Rs 350 per head, would cost Rs 1,600 per head.[11] However, for reasons stated previously, a conservative estimate has been accepted. From the same source, the cost of rural housing has been taken at Rs 200 per head, and the costs of water supply and sanitation in urban and rural areas at Rs 125 per head and Rs 15 per head respectively.[12]

Increased population triggers new housing in India when quarters become crowded, by and large. In particular, it is not so customary for newlyweds to move apart from parents right after marriage. In this study, it is assumed, conservatively, that children do not contribute to crowding before the age of ten. Housing expenditure per thousand is distributed uniformly over the ages ten to twenty-nine, along with the associated expenditure on water supply and sanitation.

It is assumed that 32 percent of the increase in population in India will occur in urban areas, and the urban and rural figures are weighted by 0.32 and 0.68 respectively to arrive at an all-India figure. The results of these calculations are presented as G in Table 34.

5. *Participation rates in the labour force* As explained above, the average participation rate is a weighted average of those for urban and rural men and women, adjusted for differences in the relative earnings of men, women, and children. The basic rates are as follows:[13]

Age group	Males		Females	
	Rural	Urban	Rural	Urban
0 - 4	—	—	—	—
5 -11	10.8	1.4	7.1	0.8
12-14	48.7	16.9	29.5	8.2
15	67.5	25.1	33.4	12.5
16-17	75.9	36.6	33.2	13.1

10. Ibid., pp. 250, 251.
11. P. Pant, "Urbanisation and the Long-Range Strategy of Economic Development," in *India's Urban Future*, p. 189.
12. *Notes of Perspective of Development in India*, p. 248.
13. *Factbook on Manpower*, p. 19.

Age group	Males		Females	
	Rural	Urban	Rural	Urban
18-21	89.8	69.0	37.9	12.8
22-26	95.1	91.2	41.5	17.1
27-36	96.5	97.9	47.9	20.7
37-46	95.7	97.7	48.7	26.0
47-61	87.1	84.7	34.3	20.6

Moreover, in view of the fact that the major difference in rates between rural and urban workers is in the early years and that much of the future shift of population to urban areas is expected to take place through the migration of persons in their twenties or thereabouts, it was decided that the best approximation available to future participation rates would be that constructed by using the *present* distribution of the population as weights. This gives the appropriately heavy weight to the high participation rates of rural youths who subsequently migrate to the cities, while causing little distortion of participation rates in the later years. These weights are[14] 0.418, 0.098, 0.402, and 0.082. It was also assumed that the relative productivity and earnings of men, women, and children in unskilled agricultural labour is in the ratio 100:75:50, and the individual rates were adjusted accordingly to arrive at a productivity weighted average, with persons under fifteen taken to be children.

The average age-specific productivity-weighted participation rates calculated on these assumptions are presented in Table 34 as H.

6. *Value of the marginal product of agricultural labour* The average number of days worked by adult male hired agricultural labour changed little over the period 1950-57. In 1956-57 the average figure was 222 days of hired work and 40 days of self-employment,[15] and this figure of 262 days has been adopted as valid for 1965-66.

There are little systematic data on wage rates for hired agricultural labour. The Ministry of Food and Agriculture's monthly publication, *Agricultural Situation in India,* contains each month a number of quotations on day rates for agricultural labour (male) in various locations and

14. Ibid., p. 6.
15. *Report on the Second Enquiry into Agricultural Labour in India,* p. 69

farm operations. The unweighted average of these observations for the period July 1964-June 1965 is approximately Rs 2 per day, which has been taken as the average wage rate for adult male labour. In order to convert this to 1960-61 prices, notice has been taken of the fact that much of the wage payment to agricultural labour is in kind, which suggests that the money wage must be constant in terms of the price of farm output. Consequently, the deflator has been chosen as the wholesale price index for cereals, in the absence of an index of farm prices. The wage rate in 1960-61 prices is Rs 1.43 per day, so that the average annual earnings of adult male hired agricultural labour is Rs 1.43 $\times$ 262 = Rs 375 per annum. This value, expressed as earnings per 1000, is given as P in Table 34. Although this estimate seems conceptually and empirically sound, a higher estimate of Rs 500 per annum has been included in the calculations to test the sensitivity of the results to this parameter.

7. *The birthrate per thousand persons* As explained earlier in this appendix, the relevant measure of the birthrate is a *projection* of the average rate that will hold after a generation. From the structure of the model, it is further required that the rate be expressed in age-specific fertility rates per 1000 persons. It has been assumed that the present age-distribution of fertility, relative to the gross fertiltiy rate, will continue to hold. This distribution is as follows:[16]

Age group	Ratio of age-specific fertility rate to gross fertility rate
15-19	0.55
20-24	1.44
25-29	1.60
30-34	1.18
35-39	0.75
40-44	0.30

The projected gross fertility rate used in the study is close to the middle estimate for 1980 adopted by the Expert Committee on Population in their population forecasts for the government of India. That figure was 133 per 1000; the figure used here is 130 per 1000.[17] This figure is used for all future years relevant to the calculations and should thus be taken as an average figure for those years. To convert the age-specific fertility rates

16. Office of the Registrar General, *Vital Statistics of India* (Delhi, 1961), p. xvii.
17. Office of the Registrar General, "Revised Population Projection," MS (Delhi, 1965).

from a per-woman basis to a per-person basis, they were simply divided by two. The resulting series is presented as B in Table 34.

8. *Projected survivorship functions* The specification of the model calls for estimates of the number of persons, per thousand born in each year within the time horizon, surviving in each subsequent year within the time horizon. This calls for a 50 X 50 matrix based on projected mortality rates.

The basic estimates of future mortality rates were provided by the Office of the Registrar General,[18] in the form of survivorship functions for five years of cohorts centered at the midpoint of five-year intervals from June 1963 to June 1978. These functions projected the number expected to survive into the next cohort per thousand in a specified cohort on the specified date.

The year-by-year survivorship functions were estimated from these data by a process of two-way interpolation. First, the data were interpolated by five-year cohorts for the intervening years. Then it was assumed that the five-year average survivorship functions centered on each year were representative of the functions for people born in that year. Thus, reading "diagonally" down the interpolated table, it was possible to derive by another interpolation the expected number of survivors out of 1000 people born in each year between 1965 and 1978. This involved, incidentally, the conversion of the data to cumulative form by repeated multiplication of the individual survivorship ratios.

The data were extrapolated out to 1981. No further extrapolation was attempted, because information was lacking for such an operation.

Data and Assumptions Underlying the Calculation of the Relation between Methods of Family Planning and Birth Prevention [19]

VASECTOMY AND BIRTH PREVENTION

The basic method for estimating the effect of a specified number of vasectomies is to determine the probable number of births in subsequent

18. Office of the Registrar General, "Working Paper on Population Projections," MS (Delhi, 1965).

19. This appendix is based on an unpublished paper by Eugene Weiss, Training Associate in Health Education, the Ford Foundation in India.

TABLE 35. Marital Age-Specific Fertility Rates

Age of women	A Agarwala (rural)	B Agarwala (urban)	C Kerala	D Jani-Punjab	E D. May (a)	E D. May (b)	E D. May (c)	F First consensus	F (c)	G Second consensus
15-19	0.91	0.86	0.75	0.87	0.77	0.84	1.71	0.84	1.71	0.83
20-24	1.56	1.65	1.02	1.48	1.52	1.68	1.98	1.48	1.74	1.48
25-29	1.58	1.46	1.33	1.47	1.57	1.72	1.72	1.52		1.52
30-34	1.41	1.11	1.50	1.24	1.26	1.38	1.38	1.35		1.32
35-39	.96	.68	1.31	.84	.84	.92	.92	.97		.93
40-44	.66	.28	.27	.57	.38	.42	.42	.41	—	.43
Total	7.08	6.04	6.18	6.47	6.34	6.96		6.57		6.51

Sources: A,B: S. N. Agarwala, *Some Problems of India's Population* (Bombay, Vora & Co., 1966) p. 30.
C: *Evaluation Study of Family Planning Communication Research Project* (University of Kerala, 1965), p. 36, mimeo.
D: S. P. Jain, "Certain Statistics on Fertility of Indian Women to Show Effect of Age at Marriage" (New Delhi, Office of the Registrar General, 1964), pp. 1-5, mimeo. Converted to normal 5-year age groups by E. Weiss.
E: D. May, *A Working Model and Parameters for Simulating Reproductive Behaviour in India* (New Delhi, Office of the Registrar General of India, 1964), p. xlviii, mimeo.
F: Arithmetic mean of each age group for sources A, B, C, E(b).
G: Arithmetic mean of each age group for sources: A, B, C, D, E(a), and E(b).

(a) As given by Registrar General
(b) Adjusted for infant death (D. May): MASFR + 0.1 MASFR.
(c) Adjusted for those recently married (D. May): MASFR for age 15-19 $\frac{\text{MASFR}}{.49}$ for age 20-24 $\frac{\text{MASFR}}{.85}$

years of those couples in which the husband has undergone vasectomy, and to assume that these births will not take place. This assumption does not take into account adultery, divorce, widow remarriage, failure of the vasectomy, or subsequent operations reversing the vasectomy, all of which are presumably minor occurrences. The number of births that would take place among those couples had the vasectomy not been performed depends upon the ages of the husband and wife, their fertility characteristics, and their chances of survival.

The assumption has been made that those women whose husbands have had vasectomy will be subject to the same fertility characteristics as those of other married women of their age. In Table 35 are presented ten alternative marital age-specific fertility patterns (MASFR). Four of the patterns, A, B, C, D, are taken from small sample surveys in various parts of the country. Pattern E (a) is based upon a number of surveys conducted by the Office of the Registrar General. E (b) is the same pattern but adjusted to account for a theoretical underenumeration of infant deaths. E (c) and F (c) are adjusted in the lower two age-groups to express the fertility of only those women who have been married long enough (2.8 years) for the births of their children to be reflected in the births counted in these periods. Patterns F and G are averages of the other patterns. A number of fertility rates have been used, on the one hand, to illustrate the sensitivity of the calculation to various fertility assumptions, and on the other hand to offer a calculation that can be applicable to populations of different fertility.

TABLE 36. Surviving Couples by Age Cohort

Cohort At Age	Age of woman at time of husband's vasectomy					
	15-19	20-24	25-29	30-34	35-39	40-44
15-19	1.000					
20-24	.949	1.000				
25-29	.891	.938	1.000			
30-34	.822	.862	.920	1.000		
35-39	.739	.777	.826	.892	1.000	
40-44	.655	.679	.726	.784	.869	1.000

Source: Based on "Working Paper on Population Projections," unpublished, 1965, New Delhi, Office of the Registrar General.

The figures in Table 35 describe the fertility performance of women of various ages on the assumption that they remain married. They should be adjusted for the probability of mortality of either the husband or the wife. Survivorship ratios are given in Table 36. These are based upon the data from the Office of the Registrar General ("Working Paper on Population Projections"). By applying these ratios to the fertility rates, sets of mortality-adjusted fertility rates are obtained.

The adjusted age-specific fertility rates must be weighted by the age distribution of the women whose husbands undergo vasectomy. As will be apparent from comparing the calculated values of births prevented, this is the most sensitive variable in the calculation. Unfortunately, little information is directly available on the age of wives of vasectomy patients. However, three samples have been found and are presented in Table 37 — A, B, C, from Kerala, Madras, and Meerut District, U.P., respectively. Distribution D, from Maharashtra, is derived from data on the age of husbands undergoing vasectomy by subtracting five years from the husband's age to represent the wife's age. It is not felt, for many reasons, that this is

TABLE 37. Percentage Distribution of Age of Wives of Vasectomy Patients

Age	A Kerala	B Meerut	Cª Madras	Dª Maharashtra	E Consensusª	F Consensusᵇ
15-19	0.3	0.1	1.6	0.0	0.7	0.5
20-24	8.9	1.6	16.6	2.5	9.0	7.4
25-29	30.6	12.9	31.8	17.5	25.1	23.2
30-34	30.3	30.4	32.1	36.0	31.0	32.2
35-39	22.1	28.5	13.9	35.2	21.5	24.9
40-44	7.8	26.5	4.0	8.8	12.7	11.8

Sources: A: *Evaluation Study of Family Planning Communication Research Project* (University of Kerala, 1966), pp. 104, 110.
B: T. Poffenberger, "Motivational Aspects of Resistance to Family Planning in an Indian Village," *Demography,* 5 (1968), 757-766.
C: Dr. R. A. Krishnan, "Report Regarding Follow-up of 1000 Sterilized Fathers Sent by Dr. R. A. Krishnan," 1966.
D: K. Dandekar, "Vasectomy Camps in Maharashtra," *Population Studies,* 17 (November 1963), 147-154.
E: Arithmetic mean of each age group for sources: A, B, C.
F: Arithmetic mean of each age group for sources: A, B, C, D.

[a] Adjusted for proper age groupings.

TABLE 38. Fertility Pattern: First Consensus (adjusted) = F(c)

Age cohort	Fertility rates					
	Age of woman at time of husband's vasectomy					
	15-19	20-24	25-29	30-34	35-39	40-44
15-19	1.71					
20-24	1.74	1.74				
25-29	1.52	1.52	1.52			
30-34	1.35	1.35	1.35	1.35		
35-39	.97	.97	.97	.97	0.97	
40-44	.41	.41	.41	.41	.41	0.41
	adjusted for mortality					
15-19	1.71					
20-24	1.65	1.74				
25-29	1.35	1.43	1.52			
30-34	1.11	1.16	1.24	1.35		
35-39	.72	.75	.84	.87	0.97	
40-44	.27	.28	.30	.32	.36	0.41

an appropriate procedure, but this distribution is included for comparison. Distributions E and F are averages of the other distributions.

The adjusted age-specific fertility rates and the distribution by age of the wives is sufficient to estimate the subsequent number of births prevented per vasectomy. It has been assumed that the women in each age cohort will exhibit the fertility of their age group for two and one-half years and also the fertility of each older age group (adjusted for mortality). By summing the expected fertility (adjusted for mortality) for the subsequent years (adding the column), the expected number of births prevented for each age cohort is obtained. Each age cohort is then weighted by its proportion in the total sample and then all age cohort values are summed to give the value of births prevented. An example of the calculation is given in Tables 38 and 39 for the age-distribution consensus 1-E and the fertility pattern first consensus (F(c)). The results are shown in Table 40 for each fertility pattern and each age distribution.

Reading down a column in Table 40 will enable one to evaluate the effect of the age of wife on the number of births prevented by a vasectomy. The Madras sample, with relatively young women, prevents almost twice as many births per vasectomy as does the Meerut sample, with its older

TABLE 39. Computation of Births Prevented per Vasectomy

Age distribution: consensus A
Fertility pattern: first consensus (adjusted)

Births per woman per five-year period initially in the cohort at age	Age of woman at time of husband's vasectomy (start of period)					
	15-19	20-24	25-29	30-34	35-39	40-44
15-19	1.71[a]					
20-24	1.65	1.74[a]				
25-29	1.35	1.43	1.52[a]			
30-34	1.11	1.16	1.24	1.35[a]		
35-39	0.72	0.75	0.84	0.87	0.97[a]	
40-44	0.27	0.28	0.30	0.32	0.36	0.41[a]
Births prevented, by age cohort	5.96	4.49	3.14	1.87	.84	.20
Proportion of sample, by age cohort	.007	.090	.251	.310	.215	.127
Total births prevented, by age cohort	.042	.404	.788	.580	.181	.025

Births prevented per vasectomy – 2.02

[a]Only one-half of the first five-year's fertility is taken.

women. Reading across the same line allows an evaluation of the effect of different fertility patterns. As may be expected, the higher the fertility characteristics, the greater the number of births prevented. It may be noted that adjustment (c), which raises the fertility of women under twenty-five, has little effect on the number of births prevented.

The consensus calculations show a range from 1.88 to 2.02 births prevented per vasectomy, which is likely to be the best guess for an all-India estimate. It should be pointed out that at present approximately 40 percent of India's vasectomies are performed in Madras State, where the higher values of about 2.5 births prevented per vasectomy are obtained. As the programmes in the rest of the states become more energetic and also utilise incentives, they are likely to reach the relatively younger couples as in

TABLE 40. Births Prevented by Vasectomy Operation

	A	B	C	D	E			F	G
	Agarwala		Kerala	Jain	May			First Consensus	Second Consensus
	Rural	Urban		Punjab	(a)	(b)	(c)		(c)
Kerala	2.34	1.69	2.26	2.08	1.97	2.16	2.18	2.12	2.14	2.09
Meerut	1.53	1.02	1.44	1.35	1.22	1.34	1.34	1.34	1.34	1.32
Madras	2.76	2.05	2.65	2.46	2.36	2.59	2.62	2.52	2.56	2.48
Maharashtra	1.87	1.25	1.78	1.63	1.50	1.64	1.65	1.64	1.65	1.61
Consensus A	2.21	1.59	2.12	1.96	1.85	2.03	2.05	1.99	2.02	1.96
Consensus B	2.12	1.50	2.03	1.87	1.76	1.93	1.95	1.90	1.92	1.88

Age distribution of wives

Madras. This would tend to raise the all-India value. On the other hand, as future fertility of vasectomy acceptors decreases, as it must if the family planning programme continues, the number of incremental births prevented per vasectomy will decrease. At present, one can only assume that these two factors will cancel each other.

LOOP INSERTION AND BIRTH PREVENTION

The concept of birth "prevention" through intrauterine contraception must be interpreted as the difference between the number of births expected within a specified time period in a population of women who accepted IUD's at the beginning of the period and the number of births expected in the same population within the same time period had loops not been inserted. This is true because loops typically remain in place for a finite interval of time and therefore alter the spacing of births among fertile women. The relevant parameters are the fertility characteristics of the population of women who accept loops and the distribution of time intervals in which loops, once inserted, remain in place.

The fertility characteristics of the loop acceptors are determined by, among other things, their age distribution, their marital status, and their specific fertility relative to other women of their age cohort. It can be taken for granted that loop acceptors are married, with negligibly few exceptions. It cannot be taken for granted, however, that the marital age-specific fertility rates among loop acceptors are the same as those in the general population. It is well known that among Indian women there is a pronounced decline in fertility rates with age. Part of this is due to increased pregnancy wastage, part to lengthening postpartum amenorrhea, and part to a higher incidence of secondary sterility. It is probable that relatively infertile women are less common among loop acceptors than in the general population of married women of that age group, since such women would be less likely to feel the need for contraception. The same reasoning indicates that married women whose husbands are absent, or women who are for other reasons not susceptible to pregnancy, are less likely to be among loop acceptors. One is led to suspect, therefore, that the pregnancy rate among loop acceptors would otherwise be higher than that of the comparable general population. In this study, it has been assumed that the age-specific fertility rates of loop acceptors may be those of still-fertile married women.[20]

The distribution of time intervals during which loops remain in place is also determined by a number of factors. Removals might occur through involuntary expulsion or deliberately because of discomfort, excessive bleeding, or other medical reasons, or because the women had decided to have more children. To date, there is but little evidence on this distribution among Indian women, since the programme began not long ago, but there is considerable evidence for other countries.[21] It is broadly in accord with this experience to assume that 20 to 25 percent of loops are removed for one reason or another in the first year, another 20 to 25 percent the second year, and so on. In this study it has been assumed that the loop intervals are uniformly distributed over the range of one month to forty-eight or sixty months. That is, if L is the length of time the loop is in place, in months,

$$p(L) = 1/48 \text{ or } p(L) = 1/60.$$

This implies that the expected length of the loop-life is either twenty-four or thirty months.

Another way of expressing the marital age-specific fertility rates of Indian women is in terms of the average birth intervals of women in different age cohorts, the two being reciprocal concepts. Further, some work has been done in breaking down these intervals into components: gestation period, pregnancy wastage, postpartum amenorrhea, and the average period of menstruation between births.[22] It appears that pregnancy wastage,

20. There is evidence for Taiwan that the fertility of women who use the loop is considerably higher than that of their age group in general, especially in older age brackets. See John A. Ross, "The Cost of Family Programmes," in *Family Planning and Population Programs: A Review of World Developments,* ed., B. Berelson (Chicago: University of Chicago Press, 1966), p. 762.

21. The Population Council, *Intra-Uterine Contraception: Proceedings of the Second International Conference* (New York, 1964).

22. R. G. Potter et al., "A Case Study of Birth Interval Dynamics," *Population Studies,* 19 (July 1965) 81-96; David May, *A Working Model and Parameters for Simulating Reproductive Behavior in India* (New Delhi: Office of the Registrar General of India, 1964), mimeo.; C. Chandrasekaran, "Mechanisms Underlying Difference in Fertility Patterns of Bengali Women from Three Socio-Economic Groups," *Milbank Memorial Fund Quarterly,* 40 (January 1962), 59-89; United Nations, *The Mysore Population Study,* New York, 1961.

TABLE 41. Age Distribution of IUD Acceptors

Age	Sample (percentages)							
	I	II	III	IV	V	VI	VII	Average
15-19	1.3	4.0	0.4	1.1	2.0	—	8.0	2,4
20-24	15.8	25.0	18.7	23.7	8.0	4.5	34.1	18.5
25-29	34.2	34.0	34.6	34.0	25.0	29.1	35.9	32.4
30-34	30.2	27.0	33.6	22.5	30.0	36.7	14.9	27.8
35-39	14.9	6.0	10.7	18.7	28.0	22.8	6.9	14.4[a]
40-44	3.6	4.0	1.8	--	7.0	6.9		4.5[a]

Sources:
- I. Delhi area, 1395 women; T. Poffenberger, "Motivational Aspects of Resistence to Family Planning in an Indian Village," *Demography,* 5 (1968), 757-766.
- II. Hooghly District: 5684 women, District Family Planning Office, Hooghly, West Bengal, 1965.
- III. Delhi: 485 cases, P. K. Malkani, et al., "Medical Evaluation of the IUD in India," in Population Council, *Intra-Uterine Contraception,* pp. 34-39.
- IV. Gujerat: 262 cases, 1963, M. D. Saigal, "Use of Mobile Clinics for the Introduction of IUDs," in Population Council, *Intra-Uterine Contraception,* pp. 60-64.
- V. Kerala: 152 cases, 1965, DAvid May, unpublished data.
- VI. Kerala: 344 cases, Demographic Training & Research Institute, *Family Planning News,* Chembur, June 1966, p. 5.
- VII. Madras: 1084 cases, Dr. Krishna Menon, unpublished data.

[a] Merged categories are allocated in the same proportion as in the remaining five samples.

amenorrhea, and the length of the menstruation interval all increase with the age of the women. It is therefore a reasonable approximation to assume the three intervals—gestation period plus pregnancy wastage, postpartum amenorrhea, and menstruation—to be, on the average, of equal duration. This assumption facilitates the estimation of the birth-preventive effects of IUD insertions.

Some data are available on the age distribution of loop acceptors in India, both from urban and from rural areas. These are presented in Table 41. From it an average distribution was derived by taking unweighted means, and this is presented as the consensus estimate.

Using this age distribution and the consensus fertility rate 3 (c) presented above in the section on vasectomy, it appears that the weighted average birth interval for loop acceptors is approximately three and a half years. This interval would be relevant if any difference between the fertilities of loop acceptors and other women in the population is ignored. To correct for this factor, a 20 percent increase has been introduced, resulting in an average birth interval of three years. In the calculations which follow, both possibilities have been explored.

In order to estimate the expected number of births prevented per 1000 IUD insertions, this birth interval and the expected loop-life are sufficient. Given that loops are not inserted into pregnant women, it is reasonable to assume that the expected time of insertion for any acceptor will be the midpoint of the combined interval comprising the postpartum amenorrhea and the menstruation period. Then, the insertion of a loop will lengthen the expected birth interval by the length of the expected loop-life. For example, assuming the loop-life to be 2.5 years and the average birth interval 3.0 years, the expected birth interval becomes 5.5 years. The expected birthrate is the reciprocal of this figure. The decline in the birthrate attributable to the loops is simply the difference between this rate and the original rate:

$1/3 - 1/5.5 = 5/33$

or about 150 per 1000. The *total* reduction in the number of births per 1000 loops would be this rate times the total length of time over which the loops would be in place, namely, five years. Therefore, the total number of births prevented would be 750 per 1000 loops. The tabulation below presents the number of births prevented per thousand for alternative values of the average birth interval and the expected loop-life.

| | Birth Interval | |
Loop-life	3.0 years	3.5 years
2.5 years	750	600
2.0 years	530	410

It is obvious that the duration of time IUD's remain in place is of crucial importance and on the sheer economic argument justifies considerable provision of follow-up services and care.

The calculation of the total number of births prevented in a probability sense has been straightforward enough. The estimation of the distribution over time of this reduction in the birthrate is not so simple. One of the complicating factors is that the women accepting loops are not typical of the general population at time of insertion, since few or none are pregnant. Therefore, it is probable that without loops there would be a tendency for births to peak in the next one or two years *among women of this population.* The greater the variance in the components of the birth interval, the more would the cyclical effect be dampened, but it is instructive to consider the case of strict regularity and no variance in the birth interval. If there were no variances, then births would take place in the recurrent pattern: (0, 500, 500, 0, 500, 500, etc). With loops, however, taking into consideration the expected attrition rate, the birth patterns would be as below: (450, 250, -200, 250, 50); that is, a total of 750 births would be prevented, but owing to the displacement of timing, in one year there would actually be more births in the population with loops than without loops.

Year of insertion	Number of births per thousand		Births prevented
	No loop	Loop	
First	0	0	0
Second	500	50	450
Third	500	250	250
Fourth	0	200	-200
Fifth	500	250	250
Sixth	500	450	50

Of course, this is an unrealistic framework. In fact, the little available data suggest that the variances of the birth interval are in fact quite high[23] indicating that the cyclical effect would be rapidly dampened. On theoretical grounds, however, one is still led to believe that the births prevented would tend to be concentrated rather heavily in the second and third year after insertion, for two reasons: first, during later years, a small fraction of the loops would remain in place; second, in the population of women

23. Potter, et al., *Case Study of Birth Interval Dynamics.*

not pregnant at the time of insertion, there would tend to be a hump in the birthrate in those years in the absence of loops. Therefore, it has been assumed that the 750 births prevented are distributed over time as follows:

Year of insertion	Number of births prevented per 1000 loops
First	0
Second	375
Third	150
Fourth	125
Fifth	50
Sixth	50

With these data, it is possible to infer from the present values of births prevented in consecutive years the present value of 1000 loops inserted in any year, through the simple process of weighting the former series by the time distribution of births prevented per 1000 loops inserted. This calculation is predicated on the assumption that the age distribution of the 1000 women receiving loops conforms to the "typical" distribution presented above.

TABLE 42. Clinical and Administrative Costs of the Madras Vasectomy Programme

			Annual cost (rupees)
I.	Clinical costs		
	A.	Primary health centres (137)	
		1. Medical officer[a]	6,000
		2. Surgical assistant	3,000
		3. Clerical assistant	1,500
		4. Sweeper	1,200
		5. Health education worker	2,500
		Total personnel costs	14,200
		6. Surgical supplies	2,000
		7. General expenses (20% of personnel costs)	2,840
		Total costs	19,040
	B.	District hospitals and clinics (37)	
		1. Medical officer[a]	7,200
		2. Surgical assistant or nurse	3,000
		3. Clerical assistant	1,500
		4. Health extension officer	3,000
		5. Sweeper	1,200
		6. Social workers (two @ Rs 2,500)	5,000
		Total personnel costs	20,000
		7. Surgical supplies	3,000
		8. General expenses (20% of personnel costs)	4,180
		Total costs	28,080

TABLE 42. (continued)

		Annual cost (rupees)
C.	City hospitals	
	1. Two medical officers[a]	—
	2. Two surgical assistants	7,000
	3. Two clerical assistants	4,000
	4. One health extension officer	3,500
	5. Two social workers	5,600
	6. Two sweepers	2,400
	Total personnel costs	22,500
	7. Surgical supplies	4,000
	8. General expenses (30% of personnel costs)	7,500
	Total costs	34,000
II.	Administrative costs	
A.	District level	
	1. District medical officer, 1/3 time at Rs 9,000	3,000
	2. District family planning officer, 1/2 time at Rs 6,000	3,000
	3. District health education officer, 1/2 time at Rs 6,000	3,000
	4. Clerical and other staff, 50% of above	4,500
	Total personnel costs	13,500
	5. One vehicle, depreciation and maintenance, 1/2 time	5,000
	6. Other expenses, 50% of total personnel costs	4,500
	Total costs	23,000

TABLE 42. (continued)

		Annual cost (rupees)
B.	State level	
	1. Director of health services, Rs 15,000, 1/3 time	5,000
	2. Director of medical services, Rs 15,000, 1/3 time	5,000
	3. Deputy director, health services, Rs 8,400, 1/3 time	2,800
	4. Deputy director, medical services, Rs 8,400, 1/3 time	2,800
	5. Assistant director, health services, Rs 3,600, 1/3 time	1,200
	6. Three clerks @ Rs 1,700, 1/3 time	1,700
	7. Two peons, Rs 1,200, 1/3 time	800
	8. Other staff, 50% of personnel costs	9,650
	Total personnel costs	28,950
	9. Two vehicles, operation and maintenance	10,000
	10. Other expenses, 50% of personnel costs	14,500
	Total costs	53,400
	Total administrative and clinical costs	43,76,000
III.	General contingency factor (100% of above)	43,76,000
	Grand total: clinical and administrative costs	87,52,000

[a]The incentive payments to doctors are included under a separate heading.

6 Conclusion

The preceding chapters have sketched some implications of high time-discount rates for a number of issues and concepts in development economics. One salient conclusion has emerged in each of these studies: that there exist significant, practical opportunities to economise on capital by more consistent application of this high valuation of time. In each chapter, this fact has suggested reinterpretations of conventional concepts of development economics, to recognise that the use of resources in a developing economy is not always guided by perfect sub-optimisation based on given technological and resource constraints.

The international cost competitiveness of any particular line of production is not determined solely by international differences in tastes, resource endowments, location, technological bias, and other influences separable from the working of the economic system; rather, it is influenced to a considerable degree by the quality of planning and management of which a particular sector or even a particular enterprise is capable, within an economy operating at less than perfect efficiency. Success in meeting international competition is dependent largely on managerial and technical ability and on the fitness of the policy and institutional environment for effective project planning, execution, and operation.

The issues of "balanced" and "unbalanced" investment strategies cannot realistically be considered under the assumption that future demands, costs, and input availabilities are deterministic and known with certainty and that the schedules of all interrelated projects are under complete control; rather, investment planning must recognise and attempt to minimise the risks and consequences of errors in forecasts, of schedule slippages, cost overruns, and changes in market conditions. Prudence suggests the provision of ample margins of safety in the budgeting of critical resources, including time; without these margins, "consistent" planning in the absence of perfect knowledge and control is an impossibility.

The significant infant industry economies based on learning through experience, in the area of investment planning and execution, are not accurately regarded as simple functions of time or cumulated output; rather, they are dependent on organisational and policy decisions within producing enterprises and in the economic superstructure. The related issue of absorptive capacity proves to revolve around decisions regarding the optimal mix of imported and indigenous skills needed in the investment process; therefore, apparent limitations on absorptive capacity are capable of relaxation, given the foreign exchange resources and the willingness to use them for this purpose.

The choice of techniques, as an application of the logic of optimisation, can often be formulated more appropriately as a profit maximisation problem than as the conventional, normalised, cost minimisation problem; that is, differences in the time-streams of benefits, assumed away in the latter formulations, often should determine the choice among alternatives. This study's empirical insight into choices among alternative means, however, is that in an economy operating with less than perfect efficiency the most economical choice will often be to improve, extend, and utilise more fully the existing facilities and to remove existing impediments to high-payoff activities.

Limitations on administrative resources do not necessarily impose rigid constraints on development activities. Practical opportunities exist to achieve development objectives by greater stimulation and utilisation of complementary private initiatives and institutions. In particular, judicious manipulation of market forces can often bring faster results than those limited by the growth of an administrative machinery and simultaneously free scarce administrative talent to concentrate on its indispensable functions.

In general, the optimistic conclusion of this study, that there are significant opportunities to economise further on scarce resources, should serve to warn economists concerned with development that extrapolation of past performance—in the form of capital-output ratios, input-output coefficients, constraints on savings or investment, and propensities to import or to export—reflects the operation of an economy at a given level of efficiency. It does not necessarily provide an accurate description of potential performance in the future. The conclusions drawn from models based on such parameters often include far-reaching inferences about the greatest possible rate of growth of income or the savings requirements of some target rate of increase, the scope for additional exports or import substitution, the limits to international capital transfers, and so forth. Such inferences are conditional on the assumption that future levels of performance and efficiency will closely resemble those of the past. The accounting prices implicit or explicit in such models, notably shadow rates of exchange and interest, are equally conditional. This sort of extrapolation is extremely useful and illuminating as a point of departure. It brings into focus the binding constraints, the critical problems. But, if indices of performance which are really variables subject to numerous policy influences are taken as parameters immutably fixed for planning purposes, the results can be very misleading. Misleading conclusions can result from underestimation of the scope for policy manipulations and concerted efforts to raise the productivity of existing capacity and of new investments.

Of the potential savings from better management of time, the preceding chapters have illustrated only some, and have very imperfectly succeeded in quantifying even these. Yet, even the crudest indications suggest that, in filling the gap between *planned* or desired increments to income and *actual* trend rates of growth, these savings could play a major part. Over a twenty-year period, the present value at 10 percent discount of the *difference* between the target growth rate of 5.5 percent and the past trend rate of about 3 percent amounts to approximately Rs 5100 crores, in 1965-66 prices. Over a broad range of public sector investments in irrigation and power, transport, communications, industries, and minerals, which are programmed to absorb nearly half total Fourth Plan investment,[1] Chapter 2 has shown that even modest acceleration in gestation time and utilisation of new capacity would result in significant increases in the present value of these projects. Assuming the *ex ante* rate of return on these public sector investments to be 8 percent, average accelerations of one year and of six months respectively would improve the aggregate present value of these investments by 6 percent of the capital invested. If total investment during the

196

Fourth Plan period should average 15 percent of national income, which is barely above the figure achieved in the final year of the Third Plan,[2] the present value of this savings to the economy would be about Rs 475 crores, as additional income over the lives of the projects. Furthermore, assuming a marginal rate of savings of 15 percent and a marginally higher rate of return of 10 percent on reinvestments, due to improved planning and execution over time, the present value of the secondary increment to income from savings and reinvestment would be an additional Rs 70 crores.[3] Also, much of this additional savings would be in the government sector out of the surpluses of public sector enterprises, which would finance new projects in nontradable sectors like power, transport, and irrigation, which are, by policy and by nature, largely the responsibility of government in India. Thereby, these savings might help to avoid bottlenecks in infrastructure which can act as specific constraints on growth.

Changes in foreign aid policy and programming to conserve capital on such project credits might make an additional contribution. Chapter 2 indicated that for projects with 8 percent *ex ante* rates of return, commitment of one-half the total capital requirement at the outset—as present project aid procedures tend to imply—reduces the present value of returns by about 6.5 percent of the total capital involved, compared to an alternative mode of financing which would leave authorised assistance free for other uses until it was actually needed to pay for project imports. While establishment of the general lines of credit implied by this alternative is not a practical possibility, further steps might be taken to break down large projects with long gestations into stages, which means the project aid pipeline might easily be cut in half. Even an increase of 3 percent of the present value of the investments involved, assuming the average annual level of project aid authorisations over the

Fourth Plan period to be Rs 450 crores, would contribute roughly Rs 135 crores to meeting the income gap; on this amount, the secondary increment through savings and reinvestment would be Rs 20 crores. The total is not subsumed under the potential savings estimated previously, but is additive, since those were made under the assumption of complete "pay-as-you-go" financing. Thus, the potential savings that can be crudely quantified in this sector of the economy alone are Rs 700 crores, about 14 percent of the income gap.

Private sector investment during the Fourth Plan in organised secondary industry, including transport and communications, and industries and minerals, has been programmed at about 15 percent of the total investment outlay. Many of the problems facing private investors are those discussed in Chapter 3: delays in approval of financial and collaboration terms, delays in import licensing and foreign exchange release; delays in land acquisition; shortages of critical domestic inputs; contractor or managerial inexperience; misjudgement of market growth; and so on. Many of these difficulties are amenable to policy influence, and the government of India has taken vigourous action to improve the investment environment. The potential payoff of these and future steps in the same direction is, again, substantial: assuming the *ex ante* rate of return of such private sector investments to be 15 percent, a reduction in the times required for completion and attainment of full capacity operations of six months apiece, would result—on the basis of calculations similar to those above—in savings of approximately 7 percent of the capital invested, or roughly Rs 150 crores. The secondary income effect would be at least another Rs 25 crores. Taken together, these results suggest that better management of time in new investment projects alone might contribute as much as one-fifth of the deficiency in the rate of growth of income. This conclusion is strengthened by consideration of another facet of the time problem in the investment field. In some potentially profitable areas for public and private investment, especially in resource fields like ground and surface water development, forestry, oil and natural gas, and copper, sulphate, phosphates, and other minerals, progress has been limited by the pace of exploration, preinvestment survey, or project definition. For some of these, heavy maintenance imports have continued despite what appears to be probably substantial indigenous resource endowments. Acceleration of preinvestment work might open up inframarginal avenues not only for indigenous capital but also for foreign commercial or noncommercial investment as well.

The main burden of the argument in Chapter 4 rests on the recognition that high rates of time discount should focus attention on the ways to increase the productivity of existing capacities. Quantification of such possibilities for any broad sector of the economy, let alone the entire economy, is an impossibility. The range of problems—and opportunities—is as broad as the range of marketing, production, inventory, financial, labour, or managerial problems that might beset any individual enterprise. Investigations in this area have focussed too narrowly on one aspect of the complex, elimination of excess capacity, largely because it is ostensibly measurable across a broad range of activity (although this measurability is largely an illusion). A more realistic formulation would replace *un*utilised capacity with *under*utilised capacity, to emphasise the general problem of increasing productivity and also maximising the value of available resources. Moreover, as Chapter 2 has suggested, the concept of a fixed capacity is inadequate to convey the possible advantages of retiring obsolete facilities kept in operation by market distortions, encouraging and facilitating substantial

TABLE 43. Idle Capacity and Value Added in Organised Secondary
Industry, 1965-1966
(In millions of rupees at 1960-61 prices)

Industry group	Idle capacity percent of 1965-66 output	Value added, 1965-66	Indicated potential increase in value added
Sugar	nil	548	nil
Tea	n.a.	410	n.a.
Salt	n.a.	51	n.a.
Cigarettes, other tobacco products	nil	157	nil
Other food products	41	281	126
Cotton cloth, mill	6	1406	84
Cotton yarn	nil	711	nil
Woollen fabrics	336	43	143
Jute manufactures	nil	442	nil
Other textiles	15	386	58
Auto tyres	30	158	43
Other tyres	n.a.	48	n.a.
Other rubber, leather goods	n.a.	166	n.a.
Paper and paperboard	23	235	54
Newsprint	nil	8	nil
Plywood	43	32	14
Matches	2	47	1
Chemical pulp, staple fibre, filament	nil	210	nil
Other paper, wood products	n.a.	385	n.a.
Cement	11	195	21
Glass	98	58	57
Petroleum products	6	362	29
Refractories	4	41	2

TABLE 43. (Continued)

Industry group	Idle capacity, percent of 1965-66 output	Value added, 1965-66	Indicated potential increase in value added
Asbestos goods	nil	43	nil
Other nonmetallic mineral products	n.a.	123	n.a.
Fertiliser (N)	152	59	88
Fertiliser (P_2O_5)	109	30	33
Sulphuric acid	78	32	25
Nitric acid	nil	7	nil
Caustic soda	27	50	14
Soda ash	10	41	4
Chlorine	60	7	4
Calcium carbide	17	16	3
Titanium dioxide	n.a.	5	n.a.
Sodium hydrosulphite	66	6	4
Oxygen	89	10	9
Acetylene	118	3	3
Alcohol	52	10	5
Benzene	52	3	1
Acetic acid	n.a.	n.a.	n.a.
Carbon black	n.a.	5	n.a.
Formaldehyde	n.a.	4	n.a.
Other organic chemicals	n.a.	31	n.a.
Pesticides and weedicides	20	17	3
Dyestuffs	43	41	18
Drugs and pharmaceuticals	n.a.	495	n.a.
Plastics	neg.	35	neg.
Synthetic fibres	n.a.	7	n.a.
Synthetic rubber	131	14	18
Paints, etc.	45	51	23
Soap	43	104	44
Cosmetics	n.a.	51	n.a.
Other chemicals	n.a.	104	n.a.

TABLE 43. (Continued)

Industry group	Idle capacity, percent of 1965-66 output	Value added, 1965-66	Indicated potential increase in value added
Finished steel	13	657	85
Steel castings, forgings	22	18	4
Steel pipes and tubes	34	54	18
Pig iron	n.a.	130	n.a.
Grey iron castings	93	47	43
Cast iron pipes	24	42	10
Aluminium	44	6	3
Copper	neg.	n.a.	neg.
Zinc	260	32	83
Nonferrous alloys	n.a.	22	n.a.
Aluminium sheets	n.a.	11	n.a.
Brass, copper, semi-finished	n.a.	2	n.a.
Zinc sheets	n.a.	33	n.a.
Ferromanganese	n.a.	5	n.a.
Ferrosilicon	n.a.	33	n.a.
Alloy and special steel	42	104	45
Structural fabrications	85	8	6
Razor blades	29	4	1
Steel furniture	n.a.	19	n.a.
Steel utensils	n.a.	37	n.a.
Others	n.a.	219	n.a.
Turbogenerators, steam		neg.	20
Turbogenerators, hydro		neg.	15
Transformers, under 33 kva	9	50	5
Transformers, over 66 kva	100	7	7
Motors	11	50	5
Meters, house	8	32	3
Switchgear, etc.	6	68	4
VIR and PVC cables	59	55	25
ACSR conductors	62	15	9

TABLE 43. (Continued)

Industry group	Idle capacity, percent of 1965-66 output	Value added, 1965-66	Indicated potential increase in value added
Winding wires	27	17	5
Paper-insulated cables	37	20	7
Dry core cables	n.a.	5	n.a.
Arc electrodes	33	16	5
Air conditioners	82	13	10
Refrigerators	nil	21	nil
Fans	33	50	15
Dry batteries	nil	37	nil
Storage batteries	nil	26	nil
Lamps, etc.	nil	20	nil
Others	n.a.	123	n.a.
RR coaches	n.a.	99	n.a.
RR wagons	36	231	77
Steam locomotives	34	40	15
Diesel and electrical locomotives	n.a.	43	n.a.
Commercial vehicles	76	210	160
Cars, jeeps	22	84	16
Motorcycles, etc.	200	21	42
Auto ancillaries	n.a.	196	n.a.
Bicycles, complete	11	61	5
Bicycle parts	nil	48	nil
Shipbuilding	n.a.	46	n.a.
Others	n.a.	574	n.a.
Mining machinery	543	14	75
Textile machinery	43	110	47
Sugar machinery	100	23	23
Cement machinery	471	14	66
Paper machinery	250	9	22
Chemical machinery	6	34	2
Metallurgical machinery	n.a.	26	n.a.
Dairy machinery	207	8	4

TABLE 43. (Continued)

Industry group	Idle capacity, percent of 1965-66 output	Value added, 1965-66	Indicated potential increase in value added
Tea machinery	36	3	1
Construction machinery	39	5	2
Boilers	11	18	2
Agricultural tractors	168	24	40
Diesel tractors	18	76	17
Powered pumps	nil	208	nil
Air compressors	122	10	12
Machine tools	30	120	40
Instruments	375	41	153
Ballbearings, etc.	200	12	24
Bolts, nuts, etc.	86	24	21
Cranes	70	20	14
Typewriters	12	10	1
Sewing machines	nil	24	nil
Watches, etc.	100	14	15
Others	n.a.	276	n.a.
Miscellaneous	n.a.	100	n.a.
Total		12906	2262

Sources: Value added figures were taken from the Government of India, Planning Commission, Perspective Planning Division, *Draft Fourth Plan Material and Financial Balances* (Delhi, 1966), pp. 15ff. Ratios of production to capacity were derived from two sources: Ministry of Industry, *Annual Report, 1965-66,* (Delhi, 1966), appendix; Government of India, Planning Commission, *Fourth Five Year Plan: A Draft Outline* (Delhi, 1966), p. 289-290.

additions to capacity at marginal expense through "balancing" investments, more intensive shift operation, reduced down-time, and so on. Nevertheless, in order to establish in broad magnitude the potential contribution of improved operation of existing facilities, Table 43 perpetuates this excessively narrow formulation and presents estimates of idle capacity in various sectors along with data on 1965-66 levels of value added in those sectors. Coverage is restricted to organised industry, and capacity data are available for only a fraction of that. Yet the figures indicate that the additional value added that would be generated were it possible (and desirable) to utilise the capacity presently idle would imply a significant addition to income levels.

The implicit assumptions underlying these calculations are that the ratio of value added to value of output would be constant as output increases relative to capacity and that such increases in output would be, under some feasible circumstances, both possible and desirable. Obviously, some of the reported excess capacity is spurious, in the sense that it is (a) uneconomic or obsolete, (b) a statistical error due to over-reporting of a capacity or under-reporting of production, (c) simply new capacity recently completed and not yet in production. Moreover, some of the genuinely idle capacity is out of service for lack of internal demand, lack of raw materials for processing, labour problems, equipment breakdowns, and for numerous other reasons. Therefore, in the short run, higher utilisation rates might be difficult to achieve. On the other hand, the coverage of capacity data in the above table excludes more than one-third of the large-scale industrial sector, so that the figure of Rs 226 crores is but a partial estimate. More fundamentally, the excess capacity problem is but one facet of the general problem of raising productivity; there are significant opportunities for reducing underutilised capacity as well. Even if only one-third of the above figure represents a realistic estimate of the potential scope for increases in income out of existing capacity, its aggregate importance is substantial. Rs 75 crores per year, converted into 1965-66 prices by a rough 20 percent inflation, and continued for a ten-year period, would contribute almost Rs 650 crores to the income gap in the present value framework presented above. Secondary income from savings and reinvestment would amount to another Rs 100 crores, under the same assumptions as before. This represents about 15 percent of the income gap. It underscores the importance of measures to improve access to inputs of materials, parts, and components in industries in which supply constraints are binding and of measures to reward exports and to increase demands in industries in which market constraints are binding.

The fragmentary estimates advanced thus far, with appropriate humility regarding their accuracy, total one-third of the income gap. Of the remainder, a large part must naturally arise in the agricultural sector out of accelerated growth in productivity. Otherwise, even major improvements in the non-agricultural sectors would be blocked; exports would stagnate and foreign exchange would be increasingly diverted to food imports to check inflation, so that the exchange for imports of industrial materials and components would remain in short supply; production and expansions in agricultural processing industries would stagnate and reduce demands on many capital goods industries already burdened with idle capacity; household savings and expenditures on commodities other than food would suffer; in short, the economy would not continue to outrun the rate of expansion of the agricultural sector by any large margin. The role of time in accelerating this expansion above previous rates has been suggested in foregoing studies. Improvements in the supply of agricultural inputs will be of primary importance, so that lags in the development, distribution, and utilisation of new seeds, fertilisers, irrigation water, power, and credit will not occur.

The objectives of Indian planning are not simply growth in income. The underlying objective is to raise per capita incomes and living standards. Therefore, the savings in per capita income from an acceleration in family planning programmes are equally relevant. Chapter 5 suggests that a modest acceleration to meet reasonable Fourth Plan targets, which might well be attainable with greater use of incentives, private initiatives, and institutions, would contribute enormously to this goal. The present value of such an achievement would be, in 1965-66 prices, no less than Rs 500 crores in terms of per capita incomes. That is, if programme results should lag to the extent postulated, income would have to grow by an additional Rs 500 crores over a twenty-year period to maintain standards of living.

As stated by the Planning Commission, another "major objective of our economic planning is the achievement of self-reliance. Self-reliance not only means freedom from dependence on foreign aid but also involves the establishment of an acceptable minimum standard of living for the masses, and a continuing rise in that standard. With self-reliance, therefore, has been linked the capacity for self-sustaining growth."[4] This certainly does not mean that India should have to make do with less foreign aid: on a per capita basis, India has been the recipient of less assistance than other countries by a wide margin, despite the greater need, the greater problems in raising domestic savings at much lower levels of per capita income, and the greater administrative challenges development poses in that country. It certainly does imply the importance of taking all possible steps to employ most productively both foreign and domestic savings, and to raise the potential level of domestic savings by increasing the returns to past and future investments. That there are avenues for raising income at acceptable rates through internal change means simply that self-reliance is in large part the result of the development process.

Notes

Bibliography

Index

Notes

CHAPTER 1

Preliminary Issues and Summary

1. M. S. Feldstein, "The Social Time Preference Discount Rate in Cost-Benefit Analysis," *Economic Journal,* 74 (June 1964), 287-304.

2. S. A. Marglin, "The Social Rate of Discount and the Optimal Rate of Investment," *Quarterly Journal of Economics,* 77 (February 1963), 95-111. A. K. Sen, "Isolation, Assurance, and the Social Rate of Discount," *Quarterly Journal of Economics,* 81 (February 1967), 112-124.

3. One empirical approach now familiar is in J. V. Krutilla and O. Eckstein, *Multiple Purpose River Development: Studies in Applied Economic Analysis,* (Baltimore, Johns Hopkins University Press, 1958).

4. This list is derived from I. Little and J. Mirrlees, *Manual of Industrial Project Analysis in Developing Countries* (Paris, Organisation for Economic Cooperation and Development, 1968), vol. II, chap. ii.

5. In point of fact, departures from efficiency in project design and selection are almost always associated with regressive income redistribution, which arises through the influence of special interests on the allocative machinery. Given the present state of the world, any movement towards larger efficiency benefits is a move toward a more equitable distribution of income.

6. L. Lefeber, "Planning in a Surplus Labor Economy," *American Economic Review,* 58 (June 1968), 343-373.

7. S. A. Marglin, "The Political Economy of Surplus Labor," mimeo., Harvard University, Library of the Littauer Center for Public Administration, 1969.

CHAPTER 2

Gestation Lags and the Rate of Return to Investment

1. *Economic Times,* India, Nov. 11, 1963.
2. The coverage of these figures includes, in general, aid from Consortium and Rupee Payment Area countries; it excludes U.S.A. P.L. 480 and TCA assistance, Colombo Plan grants, Canadian Wheat loans, and a number of minor credits for which data are not available. The concepts of project and nonproject credits are often indistinct, owing largely to uncertainty as to what constitutes a "project." In this compilation, everything not obviously in the category of nonproject assistance was considered project assistance. The interpretation of utilisation statistics requires some knowledge of foreign aid terminology and procedures. "Authorisation" generally means the conclusion of a loan agreement, itself the culmination of a process of study and discussion. "Utilisation" generally means a draft on the available funds, either in direct payment to suppliers or in reimbursement to the Indian exchequer after payment out of free foreign exchange. Thus, utilisation depends in part on the length of the delivery period and the payment terms quoted by suppliers and lags behind placement of *orders* under foreign credits. On the other hand, in the interests of rapid "utilisation," Indian enterprises have at times placed orders prematurely, with the result that equipment lay at the site for considerable periods before installation and commissioning, so that "utilisation" is not coterminous with completion of the productive facility. Some of the entries on annual utilisation are approximate, owing to changes in the terminal dates (e.g., between fiscal and calendar year) in the underlying sources, for which no adjustment has been made.
3. Government of India, Ministry of Finance, *Report of the Committee on the Utilisation of Foreign Aid* (Delhi, 1964).
4. Some of the distinctive problems in estimating capacity and its utilisation are (*a*) in many industries, the high degree of effective protection has permitted the survival of firms that would be uneconomic in a more competitive setting, so that capacity is a function of price; (*b*) foreign exchange bottlenecks and restrictive industrial licensing have hindered many firms from achieving a balanced capacity, so that large incremental output would be possible with small additional investment, or with relaxations on the equipment, materials, or processes available. The concept of capacity as an inelastic barrier to output is singularly inappropriate; (*c*) since installed capacity has been an important criterion in the allocation of scarce materials and foreign exchange and since the allocating agency has also been responsible for collecting statistics on capacity and its utilisation, a considerable degree of "gaming" has entered into the reporting process.

5. The offical data sources are, primarily, *Monthly Statistics of Production in Selected Industries* (Delhi, Central Statistical Office), *Annual Reports,* various ministries; Tariff Commission, various reports.

Other studies include: Indian Engineering Association, *Annual Report,* (Calcutta, 1964), and other special studies; A. J. Bose, *Implications of Capacity Utilisation: A Study of the Calcutta Metropolitan District* (Calcutta, Calcutta Metropolitan Planning Organisation, 1964); International Perspective Planning Team, *Report on the Development of Small-Scale Industry in India* (Delhi, Ford Foundation, 1964); J. K. Sengupta and A. K. Sen, *India's Economic Growth* (Calcutta, Post-Graduate Book Mart, 1961); S. P. Nag, *Factors Determining Utilisation of Installed Capacity in the Textile Industry in India* (Delhi, Institute of Economic Growth, 1961); M. Budin and S. Paul, "Utilisation of Industrial Capacity in India," *Indian Economic Journal,* 9 (July 1961) 19-47; R. S. Rao, "Capacity Utilisation in the Sugar Industry in Mahrashtra," unpublished, Gokhale Institute, 1965; V. K. Ramuswami and D. G. Pfoutz, "Utilisation of Industrial Capacity: A Joint Pilot Study," unpublished, U.S. Agency for International Development (Delhi 1965).

6. *Investments for Capacity Expansion,* ed. Alan Manne (Cambridge, Mass., MIT Press, 1967) p. 124 ff., presents estimates of cost differentials between partial oxidation and steam reformation and for economies of scale in nitrogenous fertiliser production.

7. O. K. Ghosh (Chief Financial Advisor, Fertiliser Corporation of India), "Problems of Financing Fertiliser Projects in the Public Sector," paper presented to the Fertiliser Association of India, Seminar on the Cost and Financing of Fertiliser Production (Delhi, December 1966).

8. The most influential exponent of this view is, of course, A. O. Hirschman, *The Strategy of Economic Development,* (New Haven, Conn., Yale University Press, 1958).

9. See E. S. Mason, *On the Appropriate Size of a Development Program,* Harvard University, Center for International Affairs, Occasional Paper no. 8 (Cambridge, Mass., 1964).

10. This is a fact that seems to impress itself more strongly on management consultants and operations research specialists than on general economists. However, for one statement recognizing this phenomenon, see H. Leibenstein, "Allocative Efficiency vs. X-Efficiency," *American Economic Review,* 56 (June 1966), 392-415.

11. William A. Johnson, *The Steel Industry of India* (Cambridge, Mass., Harvard University Press, 1966).

12. Ibid., p. 264, for the basıc data underlying this calculation.

13. GOI, Cabinet Secretariat, Bureau of Public Enterprises, *Annual Report on the Working of Industrial and Commercial Enterprises of the Central Government for the Year 1964-5* (Delhi, 1966), p. 33. This corresponds to the one million ton stage in their expansion.

14. The real burden of excess labour in such undertakings is the added *capital* cost involved in providing townships and related facilities, which average 20 percent of total project costs for major industrial projects in India.

15. *Investments for Capacity Expansion.*

16. Ibid., p. 171 ff.

17. Ibid., chap. vii and p. 232.

18. *Times of India,* Nov. 24, 1966, quoting the Minister of Petroleum and Chemicals in Parliament. For analysis of future projects, of course, it might be quite inadvisable to extrapolate this price.

CHAPTER 3

The Pace of Infant Industry Economies

1. Harry Johnson, *Economic Policies toward Less Developed Countries* (Washington, D.C., Brookings Institution, 1967), pp. 183-184.

2. Most of these studies are associated with the work of Professor Hollis Chenery. For example, H. Chenery and A. Strout, "Foreign Assistance and Economic Development," *American Economic Review,* 56 (September 1966) 679-733; H. Chenery and I. Adelman, "Foreign Aid and Economic Development: The Case of Greece," *Review of Economics and Statistics,* 48 (February 1966) 1-19; H. Chenery and A. MacEwan, "Optimal Patterns of Growth and Aid: The Case of Pakistan," in I. Adelman and E. Thorbecke, *The Theory and Design of Economic Development* (Baltimore, Johns Hopkins University Press, 1966).

3. I am grateful to the numerous officers of the Fertiliser Corporation of India who cooperated in this study and to the Managing Director, Mr. Satish Chandra, for permission to undertake it.

4. Some relevant case studies will be found in the bibliography under the heading "Case Studies on the Administration of Public Sector Projects."

5. The operation of controls over distribution in many key sectors has greatly complicated the job of forecasting demand. When available supplies are allocated administratively and all demands are not met in full, there is a strong tendency for indents or orders on the controlling agency to be considerably inflated. See, for example, GOI, Planning Commission, *Programmes of Industrial Development, 1961-66* (Delhi, 1962): "The following table indicates the indents placed and the allotments of cement during the period of the Second Five Year Plan. The indents placed by consumers in the scarcity years seem to have been inflated, since with the easy supply conditions of cement in 1958-9 and 1959-60, these have come down to a considerable extent."

Year	Indents (lakh tons[*])	Allotments
1956-7	125.39	58.65
1957-8	127.82	65.48
1958-9	86.10	72.41
1959-60	79.02	79.02
1960-1	107.16	83.76

[*]Lakh = 100 thousand.

Johnson has also estimated that in the steel industry, no less than 15 to 20 percent of the total apparent demand for Indian steel during the Second Five Year Plan period was artificial: William Johnson, *Steel Industry of India,* chap. vii.

6. GOI, Ministry of Production, *Report of the Fertiliser Production Committee* (Delhi, 1965), pp. 113-115.

7. This policy of horizontal integration has been pursued in most public sector industries, including steel, machine tools, heavy engineering, and petroleum refining. It is apparently not considered equally applicable to the private sector, out of concern for private monopolies and concentration of economic power. See GOI, *Report of the Monopolies Enquiry Committee* (Delhi, 1965), chap. vii.

8. This approach has already been recommended by the Planning Commission: "As the rapid development of the fertiliser industry has required the acquisition and training of large numbers of technical people, it would appear more economical to train new people in the relatively different tasks of plant operation. Within FCI, with the large expansion programme presently envisaged, the available talent and experience gained on past construction work could be collected in a separate Construction Wing, responsible for the planning and construction of new fertiliser projects." GOI, Planning Commission, Committee on Plan Projects, *A Review of the Construction of the Trombay Project* (Delhi, 1965), p. 20.

9. It is not suggested that all this import substitution would appear economical at present market prices and exchange rate. There are indications that the FCI is willing to give preference to internal procurement at some cost disadvantage.

10. According to two British engineers from Imperial Chemicals Industries: "In the past, many plants were somewhat over-designed to ensure they were capable of at least design output, and this perhaps helped quoted design capacities to be achieved more quickly than otherwise. However, because of keen competition in the contracting business and the chemical industry, every effort is now made to keep the initial capital cost of a plant to a minimum. As a result of advances in chemical engineering knowledge, it is now possible to do this by designing plants

more accurately to a given specification which leaves virtually no residual margin of performance. This has the effect of increasing the time required to achieve design output compared with earlier plants, and these changes mean that the time taken for new large single-stream plants to attain full production will be longer-say, even, four to five years." J. B. Allen and E. B. Bates, "Practical Economics of Single-Stream Plants," *European Chemical News:* Large Plant Supplement, Sept. 30, 1966.

11. It is possible, of course, that Indian engineers have on occasion strayed in the direction of over-design. According to one FCI General Manager, "Over-capitalisation is contributed to by unnecessary over-specification of facilities in order to meet contingencies which don't normally occur . . . The tendency to err on the side of safety in complete disregard to cost is due to fear of any possible future criticism." Dr. S. K. Mukherjee, "Cost Reduction in Engineering and Field Costs," paper presented to the Seminar on Cost and Financing of Fertiliser Projects, Fertiliser Association of India, New Delhi (December 1966).

12. This is related to scheduling and contracting procedures of the FCI, discussed below.

13. These estimates were supplied by engineers of the Planning and Development Division at Sindri.

14. Concerning FCI projects, both the Planning Commission and the Parliamentary Committee on Public Undertakings have commented on problems created in the past by lapses in planning. See GOI, PC, COPP, *The Trombay Project,* chap. iii, and GOI, Committee on Public Undertakings, Third Lok Sabha, Report no. 6, *The Fertiliser Corporation of India* (1965), p. 40. For the public sector as a whole, the Planning Commission has written: "Experience to date has been that the majority of public sector projects have taken longer to complete than was initially estimated, benefits from them have come later than expected, the capital costs have been higher than originally planned; and consequently, returns on capital have been smaller than was expected when the projects were approved. Several studies undertaken during the past years have established the fact that, to a significant extent, cost overruns, schedule slippages, and unsatisfactory decisions on size, scope, and location of plants are to be traced to incomplete preliminary planning and analysis." GOI, Planning Commission, *Fourth Five Year Plan: A Draft Outline* (Delhi, 1966), p. 162.

It is interesting to compare this statement with Waterston's generalisation: "By far the greatest number of failures to carry out public sector projects at reasonable cost and in reasonable periods of time are traceable to inadequate project selection and presentation. Few less developed countries are fully aware of the necessity for selecting soundly conceived projects with potentially high yields, defining their scope with clarity, . . . and laying down realistic schedules for their completion." Albert Waterston, *Development Planning: Lessons of Experience* (Baltimore, Johns Hopkins University Press, 1965), p. 321.

15. Commenting on this, the U.N. Fertiliser Mission wrote: "we feel that the time has come for such matters to be handled by a single technical office. With adequate staffing it would provide the benefit of continuity and accumulated information to do feasibility studies in a short period of time." *Report of the U.N. Fertiliser Mission to India* (Delhi, 1961), p. 60.

16. A decade ago, Appleby noted: "Granted prior agreement in principle on kind and dimension of program to be undertaken and the amount of money to be made available for the purpose, specific decisions incident to effectuation are reviewed by too many persons in too many organs of Government in too detailed, too repetitive, and too negative terms." Appleby, *Reexamination of India's Administrative System,* p. 17. More recently, a senior officer of the Ministry of Petroleum and Chemicals has written: "Every effort should be made to reduce to reasonable levels the time and work spent on project study and contract review, since these efforts tend to become excessive, especially in large organisations comprising many departments. Much can be done also, by reducing administrative protocol . . . and avoiding when possible the repeated circulation of important projects through numerous ministries, departments, and committees on a chronological basis." K. N. Kasturirangan, "Considerations in Framing Fertiliser Projects," *National Seminar on Fertilisers: Proceedings* (Delhi, Fertiliser Association of India, 1965), p. 171.

17. According to one authority: "If early completion of the project as a whole is important, then control of timing in these early stages can be just as important as in the later execution stages . . . In these days of rapid technological change and keen competition, planning and scheduling probably pay off better in the research, development, and project definition stages than in the conventional stages of design, procurement, and construction." John W. Hackney, *Management and Control of Capital Projects* (New York, John Wiley, 1964), p. 106.

18. The Planning Commission team which examined the Trombay project discussed this point as follows: "It is suggested that if experience is not available in each of the project organisations to evaluate tenders, it would be desirable to build up as much experience as possible in the . . . P & D Division. The present practice of using the most experienced people in their respective fields for tender evaluation has the obvious disadvantage of the time needed to bring all such people together at one meeting on a day suitable to all." GOI, Planning Commission, COPP, *The Trombay Project,* p. 10.

19. One expression of this attitude was given in a reply to a question put to an FCI site organisation by an external body as to whether a project completion report had been undertaken: "As a practical proposition in our present system of holding the individual responsible for his mistakes, both of commission and of omission, it would be unrealistic to expect individuals who have constructed projects to come up with mistakes they have made. It is also against the basic law that no individual can be forced

to incriminate himself. Therefore, in a stage of development like ours, if we have to learn from our mistakes, there must be immunity to individuals given publicly by Government. Even if such immunity is given, it is doubtful whether individuals will come up with all their mistakes, because the individual who still has a career before him . . . may have to safeguard his reputation." This statement, although fundamentally mistaken about the nature and purpose of project completion reports, aptly illustrates the attitude described in the text.

20. The following reply given by one FCI site organisation to an enquiry by a public body into procurement and general managerial problems is pertinent: "For getting this [DGTD] clearance, a somewhat detailed specification of machinery is required, and contractors take five to six months to supply it. The clearance takes another two to three months. Sometimes, certain of the items are not cleared, and after further investigation, we find that the items, or most of them, are not available in the country or the delivery schedule of indigenous supply would not suit us. Again, we have to go to the Development Wing for their clearance, and a lot of correspondence and convincing is required to get the ultimate clearance. This naturally results in the delivery schedule being postponed by eight to twelve months. Of course, there is the usual delay in granting the import license.

"Regarding spare parts also, there has been considerable delay owing to the circumstances stated above . . . These spare parts lists run to thousands of items, and it is impractical for the Development Wing to judge on, or for us to convince them of, the necessity of each and every item. As regards the . . . project, we could finally convince the DGTD after considerable delay to issue us a blanket import license."

For a more general assessment of the problem, two studies are available: GOI, Ministry of Industry and Supply, *Report of the Study Team on the Directorate General of Technical Development,* parts I and II (Delhi, 1965-1966); GOI, Ministry of Commerce, *Report of the Study Team on Import and Export Trade Control Organisation,* parts I and II (Delhi, 1965-1966).

21. For evidence on the tendency of project costs to increase under tied credits, see Mahbub ul Haq, "Tied Credits-A Quantitative Analysis," in *Capital Movements and Economic Development,* ed. J. H. Adler (New York, St. Martin's Press, 1967).

22. The Chief Financial Officer of the FCI, characterising Second and Third Plan experience with private investment in the industry, pointed out that under the old price retention formula, markup had been restricted to a 10 percent gross margin on total capital employed, out of which interest and taxes and depreciation should be met. He summarised as follows: "Thus, on account of the high capital costs of a fertiliser plant, the substantial foreign exchange involved, and the constant vigilance of the farmer and the public on fertiliser prices, the private sector has been

somewhat shy of making commitments in fertiliser factories, and the development of new units has occurred, therefore, mainly in the public sector." O. K. Ghosh, "Problems of Financing Fertiliser Projects."

23. See *Times of India,* Dec. 17, 1966.

24. The full policy statement is presented in GOI, *Fertilisers for Food,* (Delhi, December 1965).

25. See *Economic and Political Weekly,* Dec. 10, 1966, pp. 699-700.

CHAPTER 4

Time and the Choice of Techniques

1. See K. N. Raj, *Some Economic Aspects of the Bhakra-Nangal,* (N.Y., Asia Publishing House, 1960).

2. C. R. K. Prasher, "Some Problems of Irrigated Lands," *Indian Journal of Agronomy,* (March 1965), p. 18; Government of India, Ministry of Food and Agriculture, *Report of the Working Group for Formulation of Fourth Five Year Plan Proposals on Minor Irrigation* (Delhi, 1966) p. 105; B. D. Rathi, Executive Engineer, Irrigation Department, U.P., "Distribution and Management of Water beyond Government Canal Outlets," paper presented to the Fifth Near East and South Asia Irrigation Practices Seminar, Delhi, 1964, p. 3.

3. For example, R. Dorfman, "Basic Economic and Technological Concepts: A General Statement," in A. Maass et al., *Design of Water-Resource Systems,* (Cambridge, Mass., Harvard University Press, 1962), p. 118 ff.

4. These data were supplied by the Subdivisional Officers, Fatehabad and Ratia, and by Ford Foundation Consultant in Water Management, Intensive Agricultural District Programme. Equivalent full supply days are calculated as the total monthly flow at the head divided by the authorised full supply (daily) discharge capacity.

5. See Government of India, Committee on Plan Projects, *Report on State Tubewells, (Punjab)* (Delhi, 1962), p. 13 ff.

6. V. S. Baliga, "Economics of Well Irrigation in Bangalore District," *Agricultural Situation in India,* vol. 20, no. 2 (May 1965), found a differential in sales value of Rs 2570 per acre between land irrigated by well and unirrigated land in Bangalore District, Mysore State. T. S. Yeswanthi, "Economics of Well Irrigation--II," *Agricultural Situation in India,* vol. 20, no. 2 (May 1965), found an increase of Rs 215 per acre in the net value added on land irrigated by tubewell over unirrigated land in Madras State, and an increase in land value of Rs 2200-4800 per acre. The Government of India, Research Programmes Committee, *Criteria for Appraising the Feasibility of Irrigation Projects in India* (Delhi, 1964),

reported that in studies sponsored by them, land value differentials in canal irrigated areas between commanded and uncommanded areas were Rs 815 in the Gang Canal area, Rs 1115 per acre under the Tribeni Canal, and Rs 640 per acre in the Cauvery-Mettur system. See pp. 42-43. The studies referred to were carried out in 1958-59.

7. W. David Hopper, "Planning Yardsticks for Fertiliser and Irrigation," *Agricultural Situation in India,* 20 (September 1965), 468, roughly estimated per-acre benefits at about Rs 115 per acre, based on nationwide cross-section and time series regression analyses.

8. Ibid., p. 468; and National Council for Applied Economic Research, *Factors Affecting Fertiliser Consumption* (Delhi, 1965).

9. GOI, Research Programmes Committee, *Criteria,* pp. 31-32.

10. GOI, Planning Commission, *The Fourth Five Year Plan, A Draft Outline* (Delhi, 1966), pp. 217-218.

11. GOI, *Report of the Joint Working Group of the Ministries of Food and Agriculture and Irrigation and Power for the Formulation of Fourth Plan Proposals on Problems of Irrigation Potential and Water Management* (Delhi, 1966).

12. Government of Punjab, Economic and Statistical Advisor, *Statistical Abstract of the Punjab* (Chandigarh, 1966), p. 108.

13. A. M. Michael, R. M. Reeser, and G. C. Knierin, "How to Improve Irrigation Farming in India," *Extension Bulletin No. 2,* University of Udaipur, College of Agriculture (Jobner, March 1965), p. 15.

14. GOI, Planning Commission, Committee on Plan Projects, *Report on Optimum Utilisation of Irrigation Potential* (Delhi, 1965); *Report on Minor Irrigation Works* (by state), (Delhi, 1959-65). GOI, Planning Commission, Programme Evaluation Organisation, *Evaluation of Major Irrigation Projects: Some Case Studies* (Delhi, 1965), and *Study of the Problems of Minor Irrigation* (Delhi, 1961).

15. It is possible that private cultivators install tubewells on their most fertile land, which would tend to confound to some extent these estimates.

16. The costs of irrigation by private tubewell have been studies in depth, based on a large sample of sets operating in Ludhiana District, in J. S. Bhatia, "The Economics of Tubewell Irrigation in Ludhiana District," unpublished M.Sc. thesis, Department of Agricultural Economics and Sociology, Punjab Agricultural University (Ludhiana, 1965).

17. For a rather cautious view of these issues, see GOI, Ministry of Food and Agriculture, *Report of the Working Group for Formulation of Fourth Five Year Plan Proposals on Minor Irrigation* (Delhi, 1966), pp. 81-85.

18. GOI, Planning Commission, COPP, *Report on State Tubewells, (Punjab)* (Delhi, 1962).

19. Calculated from data supplied by Ford Foundation Consultant in Water Management, IADP, collected from executive Engineer (Tubewells), Government of Punjab, Maler Kotla.

20. For capital costs estimates, see GOI, PC, COPP, *Report on State Tubewells (Punjab)*, p. 21.

21. Data on annual capital outlay on irrigation account were supplied by the Bhakra-Beas Control Board, Delhi. The use of an accounting allocation of joint capital costs is not legitimate, of course, in project analysis but may be defended as a means of finding a broad estimate of irrigation costs. If anything, the accounting procedures used in the allocation of costs tend to favor power generation rather than irrigation. The cost index was derived from Government of India, Ministry of Irrigation and Power, Central Water and Power Commission, *Bulletin of Costs on River Valley Projects* (Delhi, 1960), and extended to 1965-66 using the given weights, wholesale prices index, and wage rates index.

22. GOI, Planning Commission, *The Fourth Five Year Plan, A Draft Outline* (Delhi, 1966), p. 218.

23. GOI, Ministry of Industry and Power, CWPC, *Bulletin of Costs on River Valley Projects.*

CHAPTER 5

Accelerating Development Programmes

1. The dimensions are well presented in B. F. Raina, *Report on the Family Planning Programme, 1962-63* (Delhi, Ministry of Health, 1963).

2. Central Family Planning Council, Agenda Notes for the Second Annual Meeting, Bangalore, June 1966, mimeo., Central Family Planning Institute, Delhi, 1966.

3. U.N. Advisory Mission, *Report on the Family Planning Program in India,* TAO/IND/48 (New York, February, 1966).

4. Government of India, Planning Commission, *The Fourth Five Year Plan: A Draft Outline* (Delhi, 1966), p. 348.

5. Central Family Planning Council, *Agenda Notes,* enclosures (3)m to (3)p.

6. See, for example, "Loops Still Hold the Field, But There Are Doubts," *Yojana,* Jan. 8, 1967; also "Bad Start for Loops," *Economic and Political Weekly,* Jan. 7, 1967.

7. This and the following information about the canvasser programme is based on a series of interviews with family planning officials, medical officers, social workers, and twenty-five canvassers from Madras City and rural areas. These interviews were conducted in 1966 by Dr. Jason Finkle,

Consultant to National Institute for Health Administration and Education, the Ford Foundation; Eugene Weiss, Training Associate in Health Education, the Ford Foundation; S. Finkel, graduate student in medicine, University of Michigan, and the author.

8. See footnote 1 to the appendix.

9. Last minute decisions of the Ministry of Health resulted in drastically and unrealistically higher draft Fourth Plan targets; e.g., 6 million loop insertions in 1966-67, which would have been a 500 percent annual increase. These earlier target figures were presented by B. F. Raina, "India," in *Family Planning and Population Programs,* ed. B. Berelson (Chicago, University of Chicago Press, 1966), p. 120; and D. V. K. Murty, "Targets for Family Planning Programmes," unpublished paper, Central Family Planning Institute, Delhi, 1966.

10. Figures in parentheses indicate significance levels.

CHAPTER 6

Conclusion

1. Government of India, Planning Commission, *Fourth Five Year Plan: A Draft Outline* (Delhi, 1966), p. 41.

2. Ibid., p. 14.

3. The assumption that the rate of return on reinvestment is equal to the rate of time discount obviously simplifies the calculation, as does the assumption that additional savings are proportional to additional income in each period.

Bibliography

A. Books and Monographs

Adelman, I., and E. Thorbecke (eds.) *The Theory and Design of Economic Development*. Baltimore, Johns Hopkins University Press, 1966.

Agarwala, S. N. *Some Problems of India's Population*. Bombay, Vora & Co., 1966.

Basu, S. K., and S. B. Mukherjee *Evaluation of Damodar Canals*. Calcutta, 1963.

Berelson, B. (ed.) *Family Planning and Populations Programs*. Chicago, University of Chicago Press, 1966.

Bhatia, J. S. "The Economics of Tubewell Irrigation in Ludhiana District," unpub. diss., Department of Agricultural Economics and Sociology, Punjab Agricultural University, Ludhiana, 1965.

Bose, A. J. *Implications of Capacity Utilisation: A Study of the Calcutta Metropolitan District*. Calcutta, Calcutta Metropolitan Planning Organisation, 1964.

Coale, A. J., and E. M. Hoover *Population Growth and Economic Development in Low Income Countries*. Princeton, N. J., Princeton University Press, 1958.

Demographic Training and Research Institute *Evaluation Study of Family Planning Communication Research Project*. Trivandrum, University of Kerala, 1965.

Fertiliser Association of India *National Seminar on Fertilisers: Proceedings.* Delhi, 1965.

Hackney, J. W. *Management and Control of Capital Projects.* New York, John Wiley, 1964.

Hirschman, A. O. *The Strategy of Economic Development.* New Haven, Conn., Yale University Press, 1958.

Institute of Applied Manpower Research *Factbook on Manpower.* Delhi, 1964.

Johnson, H. *Economic Policies toward Less Developed Countries.* Washington, D.C., Brookings Institution, 1967.

Johnson, W. A. *The Steel Industry of India.* Cambridge, Mass., Harvard University Press, 1966.

Khera, S. S. *The Establishment of the Heavy Electrical Plants at Bhopal.* Indian Institute of Public Administration, Delhi, 1963.

Maass, A., et al *Design of Water Resource Systems.* Cambridge, Mass., Harvard University Press, 1962.

Malhotra and Sanjeeva *Evaluation of the Benefits of Irrigation, Gang Canal.* Delhi, 1960.

Manne, A. (ed.) *Investments for Capacity Expansion.* Cambridge, Mass., MIT Press, 1967.

May, D. "A Working Model and Parameters for Simulating Reproductive Behaviour in India," mimeo., New Delhi, Office of the Registrar General of India, 1964.

Murty, D. V. K. "Targets for Family Planning Programmes," unpub. paper, Central Family Planning Institute, Delhi, 1966.

Nag, S. P. *Factors Determining Utilisation of Installed Capacity in the Textile Industry in India.* Delhi, Institute of Economic Growth, 1966.

National Council of Applied Economic Research *Factors Affecting Fertiliser Consumption.* Delhi, 1965.

Raj, K. N. *Some Economic Aspects of the Bhakra-Nangal.* New York, Asia Publishing House, 1960.

Rao, R. S. "Capacity Utilisation in the Sugar Industry in Maharashtra," unpub. paper, Gokhale Institute, Poona, 1965.

Reddaway, B. *The Development of the Indian Economy.* Cambridge, Mass., MIT Press, 1962.

Sengupta, J. K. and A. K. Sen. *India's Economic Growth.* Calcutta, Post-Graduate Book Mart, 1961.

Singh, B. *The Economics of Minor Irrigation.* Lucknow, to be published.
—— and S. Misra *New Benefit-Cost Analysis of the Sarda Canal System.* Bombay, 1965.
Sonchalam, K. S. *Benefit-Cost Analysis of the Cauvery-Mettur Project.* Delhi, 1960.
Turner, R. (ed.) *India's Urban Future.* Berkeley, University of California Press, 1962.
Waterston, A. *Development Planning: Lessons of Experience.* Baltimore, Johns Hopkins University Press, 1965.

B. Articles and Periodicals

Allen, J. B., and E. B. Bates. "Practical Economics of Single-Stream Plants," *European Chemical News: Large Plant Supplement,* September 30, 1966.
Baliga, V. S. "Economics of Well Irrigation in Bangalore District," *Agricultural Situation in India,* May 1965.
Budin, M. and S. Paul. "The Utilisation of Industrial Capacity in India," *Indian Economic Journal,* 9 (July 1961), 19-47.
Central Family Planning Council, *Agenda Notes for the Second Annual Meeting,* Bangalore, 1966.
Chandrasekaran, C. "Mechanisms Underlying Differences in Fertility Patterns of Bengali Women from Three Socio-Economic Groups," *Millbank Memorial Fund Quarterly,* 40 (January 1962), 59-89.
Dandekar, K. "Vasectomy Camps in Maharashtra," *Population Studies,* 17 (November 1963), 147-154.
Economic and Political Weekly, January 7, 1967, and December 10, 1966.
Economic Times (Bombay), November 11, 1963.
Enke, S. "The Gains to India from Population Control," *Review of Economics and Statistics,* 62 (May 1960), 175.
—— "The Economics of Population Control," *Economic Journal,* 76 (March 1966), 44.
Feldstein, M. S. "The Social Time Preference Discount Rate in Cost-Benefit Analysis," *Economic Journal* 74 (June 1964), 287-304.
Ghosh, O. K. "Problems of Financing Fertiliser Projects in the Public Sector," paper presented to the Seminar on the Cost and Financing of Fertiliser Projects, Fertiliser Association of India, New Delhi, December 1966.

Harberger, A. "Cost-Benefit Analysis and Economic Growth," *Economic Weekly,* 14 (February 1962), 203 ff.

Hartman, L. N., and R. L. Anderson. "Estimating the Value of Irrigation Water from Farm Sales Data in North-Eastern Colorado," *Journal of Farm Economics,* 44 (February 1962), 207-212.

Hopper, W. D. "Planning Yardsticks for Fertiliser and Irrigation," *Agricultural Situation in India,* 20 (September 1965), 468.

Indian Engineering Association, *Annual Report,* Calcutta, 1964.

Knierin, G. C. A.M. Michael, and R. M. Reeser. "How to Improve Irrigation Farming in India," *Extension Bulletin No. 2,* University of Udaipur, College of Agriculture, Jobner, March 1965.

Leibenstein, H. "Allocative Efficiency and X-Efficiency," *American Economic Review,* 56 (June 1966), 392-415.

Marglin, S. A. "The Social Rate of Discount and the Optimal Rate of Investment," *Quarterly Journal of Economics,* 77 (February 1963), 95-111.

Mohammed, G. "Development of Irrigated Agriculture in East Pakistan," *Pakistan Development Review,* 6 (Autumn 1966), 315-375.

Mukherjee, S. K. "Cost Reduction in Engineering and Field Costs," paper presented to the Seminar on the Cost and Financing of Fertiliser Projects, Fertiliser Association of India, New Delhi, December 1966.

Poffenberger, T. "Motivational Aspects of Resistance to Family Planning in an Indian Village," *Demography,* 5 (1968), 757-766.

Potter, R. G., *et al.* "A Case Study of Birth Internal Dynamics," *Population Studies,* 19 (July 1965), 81-96.

Prasher, C. R. K. "Some Problems of Irrigated Lands," *Indian Journal of Agronomy* (March 1965), p. 18.

Rathi, B. D. "Distribution and Management of Water Beyond Government Canal Outlets," paper presented to the Fifth NESA Irrigation Practices Seminar, Delhi, 1964.

Renshaw, E. "Cross-Sectional Pricing in the Market for Irrigated Land," *Agricultural Economic Research,* 10 (January 1958), 14-19.

Ruttan, V. "The Impact of Irrigation on Farm Output in California," *Hilgardia,* 31 (July 1961), 69-111.

Times of India, November 24, 1966, and December 17, 1966.

Yeshwanthi, T. S. "Economics of Well Irrigation," *Agricultural Situation in India, Yojana,* January 8, 1967.

C. Public Reports and Documents

GOVERNMENT OF INDIA

Report of the Monopolies Enquiry Commission. 1965.

Cabinet Secretariat. *Re-examination of India's Administrative System with Special Reference to Administration of Government's Industrial and Commercial Enterprises* (by P. A. Appleby). 1964.

Cabinet Secretariat, Bureau of Public Enterprises. *Annual Report on the Working of Industrial and Commercial Enterprises for the Year 1964-65.* 1966.

Cabinet Secretariat, Economic and Statistical Advisor. *Monthly Statistics of the Production of Selected Industries* (monthly).

Cabinet Secretariat. *Fertilisers for Food.* 1965.

Ministry of Commerce. *Report of the Study Team on Import and Export Trade Control Organisation,* Parts I, II. 1965-66.

Ministry of Finance. Department of Economic Affairs, *External Assistance* (annual).

Ministry of Finance. *Economic Survey* (annual).

Ministry of Finance. *Report of the Committee on the Utilisation of Foreign Aid.* 1964.

Ministry of Food and Agriculture. *Report of the Working Group for Formulation of Fourth Five Year Plan Proposals on Minor Irrigation.* 1966.

Ministry of Food and Agriculture and Ministry of Irrigation and Power. *Report of the Joint Working Group of the Ministry of Food and Agriculture and Irrigation and Power for Formulation of Fourth Plan Proposals; on Problems of Irrigation Potential and Water Management.* 1966.

Ministry of Health. *Report on the Family Planning Programme,* 1962-63 (by B. F. Raina). 1963.

Ministry of Industry. *Final Report of the Industries Development Procedures Committee.* 1964.

Ministry of Industry and Supply. *Report of the Study Team on the Directorate General of Technical Development,* Parts I, II. 1965, 1966.

Ministry of Irrigation and Power, Central Water and Power Commission. *Bulletin of Costs on River Valley Projects.* 1960.

Ministry of Labour. *Report on the Second Enquiry into Agricultural Labour in India.* 1960.

Ministry of Production. *Report of the Fertiliser Production Committee.* 1956.

Office of the Registrar General. "Certain Statistics of Fertility of Indian Women to Show Effects of Age at Marriage." (mimeo.). 1964.

Office of the Registrar General. "Revised Population Projection" (unpub.). 1965.

Office of the Registrar General. "Working Paper on Population Projections" (unpub.). 1965.

Office of the Registrar General. *Vital Statistics on India, 1961.* 1963.

Parliament, Committee on Public Undertakings, Third Lok Sabha. Report:

    1. *National Buildings Construction Corporation Ltd.* 1965.

    2. *Hindustan Insecticides Ltd.* 1965.

    5. *Oil and Natural Gas Commission.* 1965.

    6. *Fertiliser Corporation of India Ltd.* 1965.

    8. *Townships and Factory Buildings of Public Undertakings.* 1965.

    11. *Rourkela Steel Plant of Hindustan Steel Ltd.* 1965.

    12. *Management and Administration of Public Undertakings: Planning of Projects.* 1965.

    22. *Indian Drugs and Pharmaceuticals Ltd.* 1965.

    24. *Neyveli Lignite Corporation Ltd.* 1966.

    29. *Durgapur Steel Plant of Hindustan Steel Ltd.* 1966.

    30. *Bhilai Steel Plant of Hindustan Steel Ltd.* 1966.

    31. *Alloy Steel Project and Coal Washeries Projects of Hindustan Steel Ltd.* 1966.

Parliament, Estimates Committee, 2nd Lok Sabha. Report:

    22. *Ministry of Steel, Mines, and Fuel: ONGC, Oil Refineries, etc.* 1958.

    33. *Ministry of Steel, Mines, and Fuels: Hindustan Steel Ltd.* 1959.

    93. *Ministry of Steel, Mines, and Fuels: National Coal Development Corporation Ltd.* 1960.

    120. *Ministry of Commerce and Industry: Sindri Fertilisers and Chemicals, Ltd.* 1961.

    125. *Ministry of Steel, Mines, and Fuel: Neyveli Lignite Corporation Ltd.* 1961.

155. *Ministry of Irrigation and Power: National Projects Construction Corporation Ltd.* 1962.

156. *Ministry of Steel, Mines, and Fuels: National Minerals Development Corporation Ltd.* 1962.

Parliament, Estimates Committee, 3rd Lok Sabha. Report:

    32. *Ministry of Mines and Fuels: Indian Refineries, Ltd.* 1963.

    35. *Ministry of Steel, Mines, and Heavy Industries: Heavy Electricals Ltd.* 1963.

    51. *Ministry of Steel, Mines, and Heavy Engineering: Heavy Engineering Corporation.* Ranchi, 1964.

    52. *Personnel Policies of Public Undertakings.* 1964.

Planning Commission, *Programmes of Industrial Development, 1961-66.* 1962.

Planning Commission, *Memorandum on the Fourth Five Year Plan.* 1964.

Planning Commission. *The Fourth Five Year Plan: Draft Outline.* 1965.

Planning Commission, Committee on Plan Projects. *Report on State Tube-wells* (Punjab). 1962.

Planning Commission, Committee on Plan Projects. *A Review of the Construction of the Trombay Project,* 2nd edition. 1965.

Planning Commission, Committee on Plan Projects. *Report on Minor Irrigation Works* (by state). 1959-65.

Planning Commission, Committee on Plan Projects. *Report on Optimum Utilisation of Irrigation Potential.* 1965.

Planning Commission, Programme Evaluation Organisation. *Study of the Problems of Minor Irrigation.* 1961.

Planning Commission, Perspective Planning Division. *Notes on the Perspective of Development, 1960-1 to 1975-6.* 1964.

Planning Commission, Perspective Planning Division. *Material and Financial Balances, 1960-1 to 1975-6.* 1967.

Planning Commission, Research Programmes Committee. *Criteria for Appraising the Feasibility of Irrigation Projects in India.* 1964.

Reserve Bank of India. *Annual Survey.*

GOVERNMENT OF PUNJAB

Economic and Statistical Advisor. *Statistical Abstract of the Punjab,* 1965. Chandigarh, 1966.

UNITED NATIONS

Department of Economic and Social Affairs. *The Mysore Population Study.* New York, 1961.
U.N. Advisory Mission. *Report on the Family Planning Programme in India,* TAO/IND/48 New York, 1966.
Report of the Fertiliser Mission to India, Delhi, 1961.

Case Studies on the Administration of Public Sector Projects

Appleby, P. A. *Re-examination of India's Administrative System with Special Reference to Administration of Government's Industrial and Commercial Enterprises.* GOI, Cabinet Secretariat, Delhi, 1959.
Khera, S. S. *The Establishment of the Heavy Electrical Plant at Bhopal.* Indian Institute of Public Administration, Delhi, 1963.
Kitchlu, J. M. "Programme Planning and Project Management," *Indian Journal of Public Administration,* 12 (July-September 1966), 465-479.
Prasad, Pramanad. "The Expansion of the Bokaro Thermal Plant," *Indian Journal of Public Administration,* 8 (July-September 1962), 348-372.

GOVERNMENT OF INDIA

Ministry of Finance, Department of Economic Affairs. *Report of the Committee on Utilisation of External Assistance.* Delhi, 1964; Ministry of Industry, *Final Report of the Industrial Development Procedures Committee.* Delhi, 1964; Ministry of Industry and Supply, *Report on the Study Team on the Directorate General of Technical Development, Parts I and II.* Delhi, 1965-1966; Ministry of Commerce, *Report of the Study Team on Import and Export Trade Control, Parts I and II.* Delhi, 1965-1966; Planning Commission, Committee on Plan Projects, *A Review of the Construction of the Trombay Project,* 2nd ed., Delhi, 1965.
Estimates Committee, 2nd Lok Sabha. Report:
    22. *Ministry of Steel, Mines & Fuel: Oil & Natural Gas Commission, Oil Refineries, etc.* Delhi, 1958.

33. *Ministry of Steel, Mines & Fuel: Hindustan Steel Ltd.: Rourkela, Bhilai, and Durgapur Steel Projects.* 1959.

93. *Ministry of Steel, Mines & Fuel: National Coal Development Corporation Ltd.* 1960.

120. *Ministry of Commerce & Industries: Sindri Fertilisers & Chemicals, Ltd.* 1961.

125. *Ministry of Steel, Mines & Fuel: Neyveli Lignite Corp. Ltd.* 1961.

155. *Ministry of Irrigation & Power: National Projects Construction Corp. Ltd.* 1962.

156. *Ministry of Steel, Mines & Fuel: National Minerals Development Corp. Ltd.* 1962.

Estimates Committee, 3rd Lok Sabha. Report:

32. *Ministry of Mines & Fuels: National Coal Development Corp. Ltd.* 1963.

34. *Ministry of Mines & Fuels: Indian Refineries Ltd.* 1963.

35. *Ministry of Steel & Heavy Industries: Heavy Electricals Ltd.* 1963.

51. *Ministry of Steel, Mines & Heavy Engineering: Heavy Engineering Corporation, Ranchi.* 1964.

52. *Personnel Policies of Public Undertakings.* 1964.

Committee on Public Undertakings, 3rd Lok Sabha. Report:

1. *National Buildings Construction Corp. Ltd.* 1965.

2. *Hindustan Insecticides Ltd.* 1965.

5. *Oil & National Gas Commission Ltd.* 1965.

6. *Fertiliser Corporation of India, Ltd.* 1965.

8. *Townships and Factory Buildings in Public Undertakings.* 1965.

11. *Rourkela Steel Plant of Hindustan Steel Ltd.* 1965.

12. *Management & Administration of Public Undertakings: Planning of Projects.* 1965.

22. *Indian Drugs and Pharmaceuticals Ltd.* 1966.

24. *Neyveli Lignite Corp. Ltd.* 1966.

29. *Durgapur Steel Plant of Hindustan Steel Ltd.* 1966.

30. *Bhilai Steel Plant of Hindustan Steel Ltd.* 1966.

31. *Alloy Steel Project & Coal Washeries Projects of Hindustan Steel Ltd.* 1966.

Index

Administrative capacity, in industrializing economies, 44

Agarwala, age distribution of wives of vasectomy patients in, 183

Age: related to value of vasectomy programme, 144-146; of vasectomy patients in Madras, 155-156; and participation in labour force, 174-175; of IUD acceptors, 196

Andhra Pradesh, 109, 135

Barauni, 58, 67

Barwali Kalan, 119, 121, 122

Bhakra-Nangal: irrigation of, 73; benefits from canal irrigation in, 103; estimated total benefits and costs of canal irrigation in, 106; villages watered by system of, 116, 124-125

Bids, evaluation of, 63-64

"Big push" strategies, as unproductive, 32-33

Birth prevention: and vasectomy, 177-184; and loop insertion, 184-189

Birth prevention values, model for, 164-171; variables of, 164-166; assumptions of, 166-171; data, 171-177

Birthrate, reduction of: economic consequences of, 140, 141-143; effect of vasectomy programme on, 140, 143-146. *See also* Canvassers; Family planning; Vasectomy

Bokaro, steel mill at, 37

Canals: irrigation by, 74-77; benefits of contrasted to tubewells, 97

Canvassers in Madras study, 133-137; qualifications of, 134; functions of, 135; mode of operation, 135-136; productivity of, 136-137; income of, 137; criticisms of, 138-139; expected benefits of programme of, 140, 148-160; chronology of activities of, 147

Capital, use of, related to time discount, 1

Capital savings: by reduction of delay, 69, 108-109, 193, 196-197; by changes in foreign policy and programming, 197-198; in organized secondary industry, 198

Chimmon, 119, 120, 121; land values in, 124

Cochin, 31, 58, 67

Contractors: selection of, 64; evaluation of performance by, 64-65

Contracts, delays caused by legal problems in, 51; avoidance of delays in, 62-63

Cost minimisation, related to profit maximisation, 194-195

Dayyar, 119, 120; land values in, 125

Delays, reduction of: by standardisation, 58; by experience in procedures, 62-63, 69

Development economics: application of high time-discount rates to, 193, 196-

233

of men in, 152; estimated total costs of, 153-154; intangible costs of, 154-160; staff for, 158-159

Water, shortages in, 73; adjustment to, 74
West Bengal, contraceptive programmes in, 132